*10-Minute Plays for Kids

THE APPLAUSE ACTING SERIES

*10-Minute Plays for Kids

Edited by
Lawrence Harbison

APPLAUSE
THEATRE & CINEMA BOOKS
An Imprint of Hal Leonard Corporation

Published in 2015 by Applause Theatre & Cinema Books
An Imprint of Hal Leonard Corporation
7777 West Bluemound Road
Milwaukee, WI 53213

Trade Book Division Editorial Offices
33 Plymouth St., Montclair, NJ 07042

Printed in the United States of America

Book design by John J. Flannery

Library of Congress Cataloging-in-Publication Data

Names: Harbison, Lawrence, editor.
Title: 10-minute plays for kids / edited by Lawrence Harbison.
Other titles: Ten-minute plays for kids
Description: Milwaukee, WI : Applause Theatre & Cinema Books, 2015. |
  Includes bibliographical references and index.
Identifiers: LCCN 2015039383 | ISBN 9781495053399 (pbk. : alk. paper)
Subjects: LCSH: One-act plays, American. | American drama--21st century. |
  Teenagers--Drama.
Classification: LCC PS627.O53 A136 2015 | DDC 812/.04108--dc23
LC record available at http://lccn.loc.gov/2015039383

www.applausebooks.com

CONTENTS

INTRODUCTION

This anthology contains thirteen terrific new plays, all with characters that are kids. All of the plays are easy to produce, and none requires a kid to spray paint his hair gray and pretend to be a geezer. All have subject matter appropriate for production in schools that will, I believe, interest child performers without offending administrators, teachers, or parents. They are written in a wide variety of styles: some are comic (laughs), some are dramatic (no laughs), some are realistic, several are not. In one play, the characters are crayons; in another, they're chess pieces. Fun!

Ten-minute plays are being done as bills all over the world—so why not in schools, too? This volume amounts to one-stop shopping. If you're a teacher who wants to work on short plays in class, or a kid who wants do a play or plays with your friends, look no further.

There are wonderful plays here by some of the finest practitioners of the ten-minute play form—playwrights such as Sharyn Rothstein, Alex Broun, Jenny Lyn Bader, Claudia I. Haas, and Mark Harvey Levine, and by others less well known but equally terrific such as Sharai Bohannon, Suzanne Bailie, and Shirley King. On the title page of each play you will find information as to how you can procure permission to produce it—which is, after all, the point.

Break a leg!

Lawrence Harbison

BABY JESUS DOES NOT KILL NINJA ZOMBIES
Suzanne Bailie

Baby Jesus Does Not Kill Ninja Zombies was first produced by Theatre Battery as part of the Sleep Is for the Weak: A 24-Hour New Play Festival in Kent, Washington, on December 15, 2014. It was directed by Allison Dunmore and featured the following cast:

AYDEN: Anthony DeLeon
SOPHIA: Andrea Peace
EMMA: Shawna Petty

CHARACTERS

AYDEN: *a 7-year-old boy. He has two older brothers, and so* AYDEN *sometimes acts and says things more worldly than his age. He usually doesn't really understand the meaning of what he says.* AYDEN *is all boy—he likes to play and pretend.*

SOPHIA: *a 7-year-old girl.* SOPHIA *is precocious, supersmart, "knows" the right and the wrong way things should be done. She is an only child. She is a copy of her mother, and the mother must be a righteous pain in the butt, a judgmental know-it-all.*

EMMA: *a 7-year-old girl.* EMMA *is easygoing, fun loving, likes to play pretend, not overly girly. She comes from a family with lots of children. She is the peacekeeper between these neighborhood friends.*

TIME

The present day.

SETTING

The play takes place in a basement or playroom in an average suburban home in middle America. A few play blocks, stuffed animals, empty water bottles and maybe a jump rope would lend a feeling of a playroom.

Three children are in the downstairs playroom of SOPHIA's *parents' house. The adults are upstairs enjoying a neighborhood holiday party. From the party upstairs we hear the refrain of "Jingle Bells."*

AYDEN: He's an elf.

SOPHIA: [*Looking at a "holiday" book.*] No. Your brother goes to high school, and elves work for Santa.

AYDEN: He says E.L.F.

SOPHIA: So your brother can spell. E.L.F.

AYDEN: Every lady's fantasy.

SOPHIA: What does that mean?

EMMA: Elves have pointy ears. Does he have pointy ears?

AYDEN: He's a player.

EMMA: Does he play soccer?

AYDEN: No, like, "player."

SOPHIA: Basketball?

AYDEN: No, like *player* player.

EMMA: Player player.

AYDEN: [*He raps.* EMMA *dances.*]

The lawn is greener on that other side, if you know what I mean.

I show you stuff you never seen, the Seven Wonders of the World.

And I can make you the eighth if you wanna be my girl?

EMMA: You wanna be my girl?

SOPHIA: What does that even mean?

AYDEN: I don't know. But being a player is cool. And I'm gonna be one, just like my brothers.

[Grabs book from SOPHIA. EMMA and AYDEN look at it.]

EMMA: Look—Santa is sliding down the chimney. He brings all the good girls and boys presents.

SOPHIA: Christmas is not just about gifts, you know.

AYDEN: Yes it is. You don't know everything, Sophia.

EMMA: [*To* AYDEN.] Come on. I'm Santa and you are my reindeer.

AYDEN: No, Rudolph, your nose isn't red, but that's okay.

[Sits on block and holds "reins"—can be a hula hoop or jump rope.]

SOPHIA: My mom says your dad's nose is red 'cause he drinks too much wine.

EMMA: [*Ignoring* SOPHIA.] Mush, you Rudolph reindeer.

AYDEN: Keep your mouth shut. Reindeer food makes me gassy, and if I poop it will fly right in your face.

EMMA: [*With closed lips.*] Good idea. My mom gets gassy when she eats broccoli.

SOPHIA: That is disgusting.

EMMA: On Basher and Bouncer and Piston and . . .

AYDEN: And Vixen and Nixon.

SOPHIA: Those aren't their real names, you know.

EMMA: We're pretending, so it's okay.

SOPHIA: If you do something, do it right. Now Dasher, now Dancer.

AYDEN: Say all the names, Sophia.

SOPHIA: I will say them if we play Mary and Joseph.

EMMA: Okay.

AYDEN: Who?

SOPHIA: Mary and Joseph, the reason we have Christmas. Hello? Baby Jesus?

AYDEN: Yeah, I know, Little Baby Jesus is really Santa's baby.

SOPHIA: What?

EMMA: That's right. Mary Virgin and Santa got married and had Baby Jesus.

SOPHIA: Uh, no. Santa can't marry Mary 'cause he is married to Mrs. Claus. Mary doesn't know how to bake cookies and Santa is fat.

AYDEN: I'm going to write Baby Jesus a letter, just in case, and tell him I asked Santa for a Minecraft Core Zombie Action figure, with accessories, and a Spider-Man Rapid-Fire Web Shooter. And that I am good and will pray.

EMMA: My brother Kyle wants that, too.

SOPHIA: Jesus says no.

AYDEN: Yes.

SOPHIA: No.

AYDEN: Yes!

SOPHIA: Jesus won't get you a toy.

EMMA: Does Jesus know if you are naughty?

SOPHIA: Duh.

AYDEN: Santa is watching you. And. [*Does two fingers toward his own eyes than toward girls.*] Jesus is watching you. He knows if you've been bad or good.

SOPHIA: Sister Mary and Brother Joseph kissed and a seed grew, and Baby Jesus came out when Mary peed in the hay, because they didn't have toilets. And that is why we have Christmas.

AYDEN: Gross.

SOPHIA: It is not gross—it is beautiful, a miracle.

EMMA: I wouldn't pee in hay.

SOPHIA: It is not gross. You take it back.

AYDEN: You can't pee a baby. That's dumb and gross.

SOPHIA: It is a miracle, so it happened. So okay, I'll be Mary. Hold my hand, Joseph.

AYDEN: No way.

SOPHIA: [*Stubbornly.*] Brother Joseph, hold my hand and kiss it.

AYDEN: I am not holding your hand for a miracle.

EMMA: My brother and sister can't sit together at dinner, because they fight. If you are Brother Joseph and Sister Mary, maybe you shouldn't stand by each other.

AYDEN: Good idea. Pretend I'm the reindeer that flies Baby Jesus to the North Pole.

EMMA: I'll be Santa, but a girl Santa; I make hot chocolate for the reindeer.

AYDEN: [*Acts out fighting killer Ninjas.*] When we fly, we are attacked by sky Ninja Killers. These shooters [*Uses hands to shoot like pistols.*] will stun them, and then we chop them with our karate kicks.

EMMA: [*Acts out avoiding killer Ninjas and fighting them off.*] Yeah, and Santa has big hand grenades. [*Throws water bottles into the air.*] That turns Ninjas into, into—

AYDEN: Zombies?

EMMA: Yeah, zombies! Watch out, reindeer—those Ninja Zombies are getting close.

SOPHIA: Joseph and Mary go to Beth and Lamb's house, not the North Pole!

AYDEN: They are surrounding us.

EMMA: [*To* SOPHIA:] You can help fight Ninja Zombies with us. Pretend you are a fighting GI Joe Santa.

SOPHIA: I am Mary, not Santa.

AYDEN: Santa, hurry. Help me kill these Ninja Zombies. They are nasty crap eaters.

SOPHIA: [*Sharp inhale.*] You said a bad, bad word.

EMMA: Say you're sorry, Ayden.

AYDEN: Why? My dad says it in the car all the time. [*Like father.*] Crap-for-brain drivers.

SOPHIA: You said it again!

EMMA: Ayden, quit saying it.

SOPHIA: I'm going to tell my mom and dad you're swearing. Mom!

AYDEN: Shhh. I'm sorry, I'm sorry.

EMMA: Sophia, it's okay. He's sorry—he won't say it again.

SOPHIA: Better not.

EMMA: Come on. Mary can sit by Santa. Look out! Over there. Here comes some more bad Ninja Zombies. Here, hold Baby Jesus. [*Hands* SOPHIA *some type of doll.*] Got him?

SOPHIA: [*Annoyed.*] Yes.

AYDEN: Watch out Little Jesus, don't let them bite you, or you're a goner.

EMMA: Sophia, he can help kill Ninja Zombies, too. He has miracle powers.

SOPHIA: Baby Jesus does not kill Ninja Zombies. You can't make Baby Jesus kill Ninja Zombies!!

AYDEN: Shut up.

SOPHIA: You shut up.

AYDEN: You want to make me?

EMMA: Be quiet. Don't you remember they promised us a surprise if we played nice down here? It's probably presents. Don't you want presents?

SOPHIA: [*To* AYDEN.] Baby Jesus is going to slide down your chimney and he won't give you anything.

AYDEN: So what?

SOPHIA: And Baby Jesus will tell Santa that you are bad, and he won't give you anything!

AYDEN: [*Shocked and appalled.*] You wouldn't do that.

SOPHIA: I would because I pray to him *every* night. *And* nothing in your stocking, either.

AYDEN: [*Almost in tears.*] Take it back.

EMMA: [*Also shocked and appalled.*] That's mean, Sophia.

AYDEN: If we play Mary and Joseph, will you not pray to Baby Jesus?

EMMA: Would you not pray? Please? The Spider-Man Rapid-Fire Web Shooter looks super cool. And if he gets it, I can play with it, too.

SOPHIA: Fine, Ayden, you're Joseph. And we pretend we're in a barn and have Baby Jesus. Emma, you're Baby Jesus.

EMMA: Baby Jesus.

SOPHIA: You don't cry and you don't go doo-doo in your pants 'cause Pampers haven't been invented.

EMMA: I still destroy Ninja Zombies.

SOPHIA: No, you're a baby, and babies can't destroy things.

AYDEN: But Joseph kills Ninja Zombies so Mary can make dinner.

EMMA: Santa gave Jesus special powers so he can help too. [*Sees* SOPHIA*'s agitation.*] But only in a little way.

AYDEN: [*Puts on a pirate patch.*] Make me dinner, Mary. Or you'll swim with the sharks.

SOPHIA: Uh, no sir, we order in. I just had a baby. You want Thai or Chinese?

AYDEN: Treasure is what I want.

SOPHIA: Take that off. Joseph is not a pirate.

EMMA: Maybe Joseph is taking Mary on a pirate ship for their honeymoon.

AYDEN: Come on Sophia, you're being so bossy.

SOPHIA: You keep not doing Joseph and Mary and Jesus!

EMMA: Ayden, let's do it and then we can play something fun. What do we need to do?

SOPHIA: We have to kneel by Baby Jesus and sing his praises. Put your hands like this, like you're praying. Emma, you're like a donkey now. [*Grabs whatever was used before as Baby Jesus.*] This is our Baby Jesus.

EMMA: [*Sings.*] "Happy Birthday to you."

EMMA and AYDEN: [*Sings.*] "Happy Birthday to you."

AYDEN: [*Sings.*] "You live in a zoo."

EMMA and AYDEN: [*Sings.*] "You look like a monkey and you—"

SOPHIA: No! Like a bedtime song—something nice. Not "Happy Birthday."

AYDEN: Hurry up, Sophia! I am dying of boredom.

SOPHIA: [*Starts singing "Away in a Manger."*] "Away in a manger, no crib for a bed, the little Lord Jesus lay down His sweet head."

AYDEN: [*Same tune as "Away in a Manger."*] "The hay was stinky 'cause what Mary did."

EMMA: [*Still singing to "Away in a Manger."*] "Little Lord Jesus a Ninja Zombie–killing kid."

SOPHIA: I am so telling my mom on you two. [*Yells up the stairs.*] Mom! They are making Baby Jesus a Ninja Zombie Killer, not miracle baby! Mom!

EMMA: I think Baby Jesus wants to be our friend and wants to play Ninja Zombies.

AYDEN: Me, too. We did Mary and Joseph—now it's our turn.

SOPHIA: You two are impossible.

AYDEN: [*To EMMA.*] Pirates?

EMMA: Let's have Sophia walk the plank.

AYDEN: Shark bait.

SOPHIA: I am not shark bait.

EMMA: Not yet.

[AYDEN *and* EMMA, *laughing, start to chase* SOPHIA *around, teasing her that she will walk the plank. Lights fade.*]

END OF PLAY

THE BIG PICTURE

Mark Harvey Levine

The Big Picture was first produced by the Malibu Stage Company as part of the Second Malibu International Play Festival in November 2002. It was directed by Michael Preece, and had the following cast:

SKY BLUE: Erin Russell
BURNT SIENNA: Rachel Tucker
LEMON YELLOW: Sondi Kroeger
COPPER: Chuck Kelley
OLIVE GREEN: Merrill Davis
PEACH: David Reiter

CHARACTERS

SKY BLUE: *9 to 15 years old; female, kind.*
BURNT SIENNA: *9 to 15 years old; male or female, shorter.*
LEMON YELLOW: *9 to 15 years old; female, skittish.*
COPPER: *9 to 15 years old; male, a bully.*
OLIVE GREEN: *9 to 15 years old; female, grumpy.*
PEACH: *9 to 15 years old; female or male, skittish.*

TIME

The present.

SETTING

A desk in kindergarten.

> *Lights up on six actors grouped in two rows. Each wears a different color shirt:* SKY BLUE, BURNT SIENNA, LEMON YELLOW, COPPER, OLIVE GREEN, PEACH. *They are crayons. They stand frozen for a moment, just looking around.*

PEACH: We're being taken out!

OLIVE GREEN: Oh, great.

SKY BLUE: How are you, Burnt Sienna?

BURNT SIENNA: [*Short, his/her shirt is torn at the neck, like paper ripped from a crayon.*]

Man, I'm fried.

COPPER: [*A bit of a bully.*] You're lookin' a little used-up there, friend.

SKY BLUE: [*Holding* BURNT SIENNA.] Don't say that! [*Pause. They stare out the fourth wall, trying to see.*]

LEMON YELLOW: [*Sweet, but a little flighty.*] So what's going on?

PEACH: Is it a picture?

ALL: A picture! Oh no! Help!

OLIVE GREEN: Maybe it's not a picture. Maybe it's just a little doodle.

COPPER: Maybe she's making a candle. [*A horrified half pause.*]

PEACH: We're all gonna die!

LEMON YELLOW: Copper! Don't say that.

SKY BLUE: Paper! I see paper!

COPPER: We have paper. I repeat, we have paper.

OLIVE GREEN: [*As in, "Oh, dear God."*] Oh, dear Debbie.

BURNT SIENNA: Please don't use me. Please don't use me.

PEACH: I don't want to die! Don't draw anything me-colored . . .

OLIVE GREEN: Or olive green. Who likes olive green? It's not a pretty color, I'll be the first to admit.

ALL: Oh right. Don't want to use me. Me, neither. Nope. Not me.

COPPER: What's the paper situation?

PEACH: Yeah, how much paper are we talking? [*They all strain to see.*]

SKY BLUE: It's . . . hard to see from this angle . . . but . . . Oh, no . . .

LEMON YELLOW: What?

BURNT SIENNA: It's butcher paper.

SKY BLUE: It's a mural!

PEACH: We're all gonna die!

COPPER: Shut up.

PEACH: You shut up!

COPPER: [*Making a grab for* PEACH.] You're a sickly little shade, Peach!

PEACH: [*Hiding behind another crayon.*] You'll never take me alive, Copper!

SKY BLUE: Guys! Guys!

OLIVE GREEN: Has she started drawing?

LEMON YELLOW: Something's taking shape.

COPPER: Is that an elephant?

SKY BLUE: I think it's a dog.

LEMON YELLOW: The hand of Debbie is subtle.

[*They nod.* BURNT SIENNA *begins to be dragged off by an unseen hand.*]

BURNT SIENNA: Here I go again. [*He exits.*]

PEACH: Burnt Sienna hasn't been looking too good.

LEMON YELLOW: He's [*Or "She's".*] just a little smaller, that's all.

SKY BLUE: Debbie's wearing a pretty dress today.

PEACH: She spilled juice on it, though.

LEMON YELLOW: The way of Debbie is messy.

[*They all nod knowingly.*]

COPPER: You're changing the subject, Sky Blue.

SKY BLUE: Well, what do you want me to say?

LEMON YELLOW: Burnt Sienna's going to be fine.

[*They notice something.*]

OLIVE GREEN: Oy, Gevalt.

LEMON YELLOW: What?

OLIVE GREEN: Ground.

PEACH: What?

OLIVE GREEN: She's drawing the ground.

COPPER: With Burnt Sienna.

SKY BLUE: I can't watch.

LEMON YELLOW: The whole ground?

COPPER: All the way across.

OLIVE GREEN: This is gonna be bad.

PEACH: No! Take me! Take me!

COPPER: [*Holding* PEACH *back, very war movie.*] Don't be a fool, soldier! You can't have a pink ground!

PEACH: Hey! I'm Peach! Peach! Peach!

COPPER: Yeah, whatever.

SKY BLUE: Look!

OLIVE GREEN: Here comes another kid . . .

[*Pause. They listen, then . . .*]

LEMON YELLOW: Well, that wasn't very nice.

PEACH: He shouldn't have said that to Debbie.

OLIVE GREEN: Everyone's a critic.

[*Pause.*]

LEMON YELLOW: [*Quietly.*] Debbie's crying.

[*Pause. PEACH puts an umbrella up. BURNT SIENNA comes back, staggers, and collapses. SKY BLUE rushes over to BURNT SIENNA.*]

BURNT SIENNA: That took a lot out of me.

[COPPER *gets dragged away quickly.*]

COPPER: Woah!

[*The other crayons give SKY BLUE and BURNT SIENNA a little space and watch the picture being drawn.*]

PEACH: Now she's drawing a big, angry stick in the ground.

BURNT SIENNA: [*Away from the others, to SKY BLUE.*] I don't think I'm going to make it.

SKY BLUE: Of course you are, you've got plenty of life left . . .

OLIVE GREEN: [*Re: the picture.*] I still don't get it.

PEACH: What's to get? It's a dog, and a house.

LEMON YELLOW: And a big angry stick.

OLIVE GREEN: I guess I just don't understand art. [COPPER *is tossed onstage. He rolls for a bit. OLIVE GREEN is dragged off quickly.*] *Vey is meer.* [*As in, "Woe is me!"*]

BURNT SIENNA: I feel . . . broken. Inside.

SKY BLUE: Shhh . . . don't say anything.

PEACH: Ohhhh . . . it's a big angry tree in the ground.

BURNT SIENNA: I think I'm broken inside my paper.

[OLIVE GREEN *is tossed onstage. LEMON YELLOW is dragged off quickly.*]

LEMON YELLOW: Here I go!

OLIVE GREEN: Boy, is she upset!

PEACH: We've got to do something.

OLIVE GREEN: She's gonna kill us all!

[LEMON YELLOW *is tossed back in. They all brace themselves, but no other crayon is taken.*]

SKY BLUE: She stopped.

BURNT SIENNA: Is she finished?

LEMON YELLOW: I don't think so.

PEACH: It feels like there's something missing.

OLIVE GREEN: She's still crying.

BURNT SIENNA: Listen . . . if I . . . get used up . . . go away . . . completely . . .

SKY BLUE: But you'll never go away. Don't you see? You're there in everything that's your color—all the candy bars Debbie has drawn, in monkeys, in root beer . . . in the very ground!

LEMON YELLOW: Yeah!

OLIVE GREEN: It's a kind of . . . immortality.

SKY BLUE: You're part of the picture. She couldn't have made it without you!

PEACH: What's the point of being a crayon if you can't be in the picture?

LEMON YELLOW: Without us, the world would be colorless and flat.

OLIVE GREEN: Butcher paper.

PEACH: She's right.

COPPER: Hey! I'm ready, coach! Put me in!

LEMON YELLOW: Don't cry, Debbie! Use me!

COPPER: Come on! I'm shiny!

PEACH: [*Throwing down the umbrella.*] Pick me!

OLIVE GREEN: Pick me! Make another tree!

LEMON YELLOW: Make the sun! [*Suddenly,* SKY BLUE *is dragged offstage by an unseen hand.*]

SKY BLUE: She picked me! [*They cheer, but the cheers slowly change to increasingly horrified expressions.*]

LEMON YELLOW: Oh. Oh my.

[BURNT SIENNA *sits up weakly.*]

BURNT SIENNA: What? What?

COPPER: She's making the sky.

BURNT SIENNA: Sky? What sky? You just leave it blank, there's nothing there.

COPPER: You don't get it, do you, kid?

OLIVE GREEN: [*Gently.*] It's butcher paper. It's brown.

COPPER: And the sky's gotta be blue.

BURNT SIENNA: [*Struggling to his feet.*] No! She'll never last!

LEMON YELLOW: We have to think of the big picture, honey.

BURNT SIENNA: What about clouds? Shouldn't there be some white clouds? How about some fluffy clouds?

COPPER: [*Quietly.*] Looks like it's gonna be a nice clear day.

[*They are suddenly grouped together, by the unseen hand.*]

PEACH: Woah . . . back in the box.

COPPER: Cardboard falls again.

[*They stand in two rows again, like a box of crayons. There is a space for* SKY BLUE, *the missing crayon. As crayons will, the one next to the space, in this case* LEMON YELLOW, *leans diagonally into the space.* LEMON YELLOW *puts her head on the shoulder of the crayon she's leaning against,* BURNT SIENNA.]

OLIVE GREEN: It's gonna be a great picture.

LEMON YELLOW: She'll always be up there . . . part of the sky . . .

BURNT SIENNA: Hey, do you guys think . . . ?

PEACH: You know it.

OLIVE GREEN: This picture? No doubt.

[*As the lights fade.*]

COPPER: Oh yeah. [*Calling out to* SKY BLUE.] That's going up on the fridge, baby! That's going on the refrigerator! Up on the fridge!

[*They all join in.*]

ALL: [*Except* SKY BLUE.] Up on the fridge! Up on the fridge! Up on the fridge!!!

[*Lights out.*]

END OF PLAY

THE GREAT
STEVEN STRAVINSKY

Sharai Bohannon

The Great Steven Stravinsky premiered as part of Texas Tech University's Raider Red's One-Act Play Spectacular in the Lab Theatre on March 2, 2015, through March 8, 2015. The cast was as follows:

STEVEN: Raymond Compton
TRAVIS: Hannah Johnson
AMANDA: Aubree May Zuniga

CHARACTERS

STEVEN: *an 11-year-old boy; he wants to be a magician.*
TRAVIS: *a 6-year-old boy;* STEVEN's *little brother.*
AMANDA: *an 11-year-old girl;* STEVEN's *friend.*

TIME

The present day.

SETTING

STEVEN's *backyard. It is set up for* STEVEN's *birthday party.* STEVEN *has a magic station, with a box big enough to fit a person inside of.* TRAVIS *and* AMANDA *are watching* STEVEN's *show.*

STEVEN: Abracadabra! [*He turns his hat upside down and a stuffed rabbit falls out, along with a handful of Velcro strips. He looks horrified.*] It would've worked with a real rabbit.

AMANDA: I'm sure it would've.

TRAVIS: Mom and Dad said he couldn't have a rabbit because of what he did to the goldfish.

STEVEN: Shut up, Travis!

TRAVIS: You can't tell me to shut up! Mom said!

STEVEN: [*He turns to* AMANDA.] That's not what actually happened—

TRAVIS: Is too! You killed Sprinkles and Sandy on accident.

STEVEN: Travis! Let it go!

[STEVEN *turns to* AMANDA *and begins to speak, but then stops.*]

AMANDA: Goldfish die all of the time. It probably had nothing to do with you.

[STEVEN *and* AMANDA *share a look.*]

TRAVIS: No. It was Steven's fault. [STEVEN *shoots* TRAVIS *an angry look.*] But he didn't mean to kill them. They're in a better place now anyway. They're in heaven because Daddy flushed them down the—

AMANDA: What's the next trick? I want to see more magic.

STEVEN: My next trick is complicated. Give me a minute to set up. [*He busies himself setting up the giant box.* TRAVIS *begins to speak to* AMANDA *in rapid whispers.*]

TRAVIS: Do you like *SpongeBob*? There's a *SpongeBob* marathon on right now. I bet if you tell Steven you want to watch it, he'll let us go.

AMANDA: I think Steven has more tricks to show us. Don't you want to see what he does next?

TRAVIS: He only has four tricks. I wanna watch *SpongeBob*!

AMANDA: Maybe after he's done we can watch some of the marathon.

TRAVIS: Are you only saying that because Steven likes you? Is that why you want to stay out here and watch this stupid show?

[AMANDA *looks over at* STEVEN *and smiles.* STEVEN *struggles to free his cape from the back of the giant box.*]

AMANDA: What do you mean he "likes me?"

TRAVIS: It's what Mom was telling Dad last night. Dad was complaining about Steven always being in the bathroom, and then Mom said, "He's at that age!" Then I heard them laugh before Mom said, "Steven likes the girl that is coming to his birthday party."

AMANDA: Where did you hear all of this?

STEVEN: [*Yelling from behind the box.*] I'm almost ready, guys!

TRAVIS: I was doing this thing called easy-dropping outside their door. I'm gonna be a spy when I grow up.

AMANDA: What else did they say?

TRAVIS: They talked about a bunch of boring stuff and then they started making weird noises. I think they were wrestling again. They've been doing that a lot since Dad got his happy pills in the mail. [*Beat.*] I was going to easy-drop on Steven, but he was still in the bathroom. Dad says that we might have to build him his own bathroom at this rate.

[STEVEN *makes grand gestures with his cape and steps in front of the box.*]

STEVEN: For my next trick, I will need a volunteer. Are there any volunteers? How about you, sir?

TRAVIS: Me?

STEVEN: You are the only sir here.

TRAVIS: But you said the next time I touch your magic stuff, you would give me a swirly.

[STEVEN *looks embarrassingly at* AMANDA *and then back at* TRAVIS.]

STEVEN: Just get in the box!

TRAVIS: Are you sure I'm not going to get into trouble? I don't want another swirly.

AMANDA: I don't think he's going to give you a swirly, Travis. He seems to really want you to get into the box.

TRAVIS: Okay, but I'm going to say I told you so if I get a . . .

STEVEN: Travis! Get in the box!

[TRAVIS *walks hesitantly towards the box.*]

TRAVIS: Which trick is this?

STEVEN: The one we rehearsed all week.

TRAVIS: Is this the one where you tap the box and I climb o—

STEVEN: Stop talking, Travis!

[AMANDA *laughs and tries to cover it with a cough.*]

STEVEN: For this trick, the Great Steven Stravinsky will make this child disappear.

TRAVIS: Our last name is Walters.

STEVEN: It's my stage name! Just get in the box, Travis.

TRAVIS: Fine!

[TRAVIS *climbs into the box and* STEVEN *closes the lid.* STEVEN *uses his wand to tap the lid a few times.*]

STEVEN: Abracadabra!

[STEVEN *opens the box and* TRAVIS *is still there.*]

TRAVIS: I got stuck!

STEVEN: Why do you ruin everything?!

[AMANDA *stands up.*]

AMANDA: I'm sure he didn't mean to get stuck. Let's just get him unstuck so you can try again.

STEVEN: Fine!

[STEVEN *pulls* TRAVIS *out of the box.* TRAVIS's *shirt rips and he begins to cry.*]

TRAVIS: You ripped my Batman shirt!

STEVEN: It was an accident.

TRAVIS: I'm telling!

[TRAVIS *runs into the house crying.* STEVEN *turns to* AMANDA.]

STEVEN: It was an accident!

AMANDA: I'm sure it was. [*She walks over to* STEVEN *and begins to rub his cape.*] I really like your cape.

STEVEN: Thanks! I brought it with my own allowance. It took me a few months to save up for it, but I needed it. Otherwise, how would people know that I am a real magician?

AMANDA: Right! [*Beat.*] Thanks for inviting me to your party!

STEVEN: Thanks for coming! I was hoping there would be more people, so that you could have lots of people to talk to.

AMANDA: This is more fun. I like talking to you.

STEVEN: I like talking to you too. [STEVEN *and* AMANDA *have a moment.* STEVEN *begins to lean into her, but abruptly stops.*] Do you want to hold my wand? It's just like the one Harry Potter uses in the movies.

AMANDA: Oh . . . that's awesome!

STEVEN: It was a gift. It would've taken me a lot more than a few months to afford something this cool.

[STEVEN *hands the wand to* AMANDA.]

AMANDA: It's really cool, Steven. [*Beat.*] Steven . . . Travis told me that he overheard . . . that you like me.

[STEVEN *gets uncomfortable.*]

STEVEN: I wish I could make him disappear for good.

AMANDA: I just wanted you to know that I know. Sometimes . . . I think you're going to kiss me and I just thought you might actually kiss me if you knew . . . that I knew and I was okay with it.

[*She begins to really focus on the wand.* STEVEN *gets more uncomfortable.*]

STEVEN: So . . . when would be a good time to . . . do that.

AMANDA: Whenever. Now is fine too. Or, whenever.

STEVEN: Oh . . . I'm just not sure how to . . . I mean I know how, but I've never actually . . .

AMANDA: Me either. We could just try it and see what happens. I mean, if you want to.

STEVEN: I want to. I really want to.

[*He begins to lean in again.* AMANDA *smiles.*]

TRAVIS: Steven! [TRAVIS *runs out of the house.* STEVEN *and* AMANDA *separate.*] Mom said she would buy me a new T-shirt if I don't tell you about the surprise she's bringing out. So, I can forgive you this time. [*Beat.*] Can I play with your new magic set when she brings it out?

STEVEN: Travis!

TRAVIS: What?

[AMANDA *laughs and gives* STEVEN *back his wand.*]

AMANDA: Let's see some more magic!

[*She sits back down and looks at* STEVEN.]

STEVEN: Travis, get in the box. We are going to do it right this time.

[TRAVIS *gets into the box.* STEVEN *taps it with his wand.*]

STEVEN: Abracadabra!

[STEVEN *opens the box and* TRAVIS *is still there.*]

TRAVIS: I didn't hear you say the magic word!

STEVEN: Travis!

TRAVIS: You said not to climb out until I hear the word!

STEVEN: Stop talking! Just stop talking!

[TRAVIS *steps out of the box.* AMANDA *stands up and goes over to intervene.*]

TRAVIS: Nobody even wants to see your stupid show. I wanted to watch *SpongeBob* with Amanda! You need to learn how to share your girlfriend—

AMANDA: Guys! How about we do a different magic trick?

TRAVIS: He's already done all of the ones he knows.

STEVEN: That's not true! I have other tricks, Travis.

TRAVIS: The other one involves fire and Mom said you're not allowed to play with matches anymore because you set the tablecloth on fire at Aunt Mary's wedding.

STEVEN: Shut up, Travis!

TRAVIS: You can't tell me to shut up! Mom said!

AMANDA: Why don't we play a game?

TRAVIS: Because Steven cheats!

STEVEN: I don't cheat! You're just not smart enough to win!

AMANDA: Travis, go pick a board game. We'll take a magic break and then try this trick again later.

TRAVIS: Even your girlfriend doesn't want to see any more of your stupid act.

[AMANDA *looks at* STEVEN *and* STEVEN *looks at his shoes.*]

AMANDA: I like your act. I think it's cool. I never said it was stupid.

STEVEN: She's not my . . . she's . . . shut up, Travis!

TRAVIS: You can't tell me to shut up! Mom said!

[TRAVIS *proceeds to lose it. He grabs* STEVEN's *wand and begins to run in circles as he pulls down decorations.* STEVEN *chases after him as they yell at each other.* TRAVIS *yells so loud and fast that it sounds like a war chant:*]

You can shut up! You can shut up! You can shut up!

STEVEN: Give me back my wand, you brat!

AMANDA: [*Shouting over the ruckus.*] Hey, Travis! If you give Steven back his wand, you can watch *SpongeBob!*

TRAVIS: [TRAVIS *negotiates with* AMANDA *without breaking his stride.*] Will you watch it with me?

AMANDA: Sure. After the magic show is over.

TRAVIS: Promise?

AMANDA: I promise to watch some of the marathon with you after Steven's show.

[TRAVIS *throws the wand down and runs toward the house.* STEVEN *picks up his wand and checks it for damage.* AMANDA *joins him in his inspection.*]

AMANDA: Is it broken?

[STEVEN *waves it around a few times before resting it against his chest in a protective manner.*]

STEVEN: It's okay. I was so scared.

AMANDA: I'm glad it wasn't broken. I really would like to see more magic someday.

STEVEN: Really?

AMANDA: Yeah! I like watching your show. I've never known a real magician before.

[STEVEN *looks pleased.* STEVEN *realizes that* AMANDA *is rubbing her arms and shivering. He unties his cape and wraps it around her.* STEVEN *begins to tie the strings around her neck and then stops himself.* AMANDA *ties the cape on as* STEVEN *fiddles with his wand.*]

STEVEN: Thank you! [*Beat.*] Thanks for saving my wand, too! It means a lot to me.

AMANDA: Glad I could help! [*Beat.*] Your little brother would get along with my little sister. She's a nightmare too. Maybe if you ever come over to my place, you could bring him with you.

STEVEN: He's so annoying! I wish I was an only kid! [*He realizes what just happened.*] I would like that . . . to come over to your place. I mean, with Travis, because he would get along with your sister and stuff . . .

AMANDA: I think she'd like that too.

STEVEN: That would be really good for Travis. He doesn't have any friends. We only moved here six months ago and the other kids in his class think he's weird.

[STEVEN *realizes that he is playing with his wand as he stares at* AMANDA. *He abruptly stops doing both.*]

AMANDA: I don't think he's weird. I think the other kids are stupid. I had an awesome time here today. I'm really happy you invited me.

STEVEN: I'm really happy you could make it. I know there was a pool party that everyone else was invited to.

AMANDA: This was much better than that stupid party. I'm still really mad they threw a party after you sent your invitations out.

STEVEN: It's okay. I'm kind of used to it . . .

AMANDA: It was still really mean. I don't like how those boys pick on you—

STEVEN: Are you here because you felt sorry for me?

AMANDA: No. I'm here because I . . . I like you . . . and I thought that you liked me, too. [*Beat.*] Also, magic is really cool.

[STEVEN *and* AMANDA *share a moment.*]

TRAVIS: [*From offstage.*] Is the show over, yet? I want Amanda to come watch *SpongeBob* with me!

STEVEN: [*Returning the yell.*] In a minute! [*To* AMANDA.] He ruins everything.

AMANDA: Steven . . .

STEVEN: I think he does it on purpose. Just to . . .

AMANDA: Steven. [*Beat.*] Do you still want to . . .

STEVEN: Yes! [*Beat.*] I mean . . . if you still want to.

AMANDA: I still want to.

[*She looks at him expectantly. It takes* STEVEN *a moment to realize what is happening.*]

STEVEN: Oh! Like . . . do you want to do that now?

[AMANDA *nods her head.* STEVEN *begins to lean in. They share an awkward kiss.*]

STEVEN: Was that okay?

[AMANDA *wraps herself in the cape and smiles.*]

AMANDA: It was very okay.

STEVEN: Thank you . . . I mean . . .

[AMANDA *giggles.*]

AMANDA: We should go inside before Travis gets mad again.

[*She holds her hand out.* STEVEN *takes a moment to figure out what is going on. He eagerly grabs her hand and begins to follow her into the house.*]

TRAVIS: [*From offstage.*] What are you guys doing out there? You're missing the best part!

[*Lights fade.*]

END OF PLAY

THE GUPPY BALLET
A Dance Play
Lawrence Thelen

The Guppy Ballet premiered at the Newburgh Free Academy in Newburgh, New York, in 2009. Terry Sandler was the producer.

CHARACTERS
Four guppies of the same school:
DORSAL: *the head fish*
GILL: *the middle fish*
HERRY: *the bottom fish*
ROXANNE: *the youngest fish*

TIME
The present day.

SETTING
The middle of the sea.

NOTE: THE GUPPY BALLET *can be performed with or without music, depending on whether it is being presented as a pantomime or as a choreographed dance-play. All in all, the swimming sections are elongated sequences and should not be rushed.*

Just as fish swim in harmonious synchronization due to their highly developed sense of sonar, so too do the characters in this play move (or swim.) as one. They are, in essence, a single character, until . . . well, you'll see.

As the lights come up, the fish swim. They dart, dive, glide, and dance as one. The motion is simultaneously beautiful, mesmerizing, and oddly unsettling in its precision. After a moment, DORSAL, the head fish, comes upon a morsel, eats it, and exclaims to the others with glee:

DORSAL: Seaweed spores!

[A brief feeding frenzy ensues. Once the food is devoured, the fish swim in exuberant, synchronized happiness. The exultation eventually fades back into the day-to-day exploration for food. They swim as one. After a moment, GILL, the middle fish, comes upon a morsel, eats it, and exclaims to the others with glee:]

GILL: Shrimp roe!

HERRY: Shrimp roe?

GILL: Shrimp roe!

[*Once again, a brief feeding frenzy ensues. And again, after the food is devoured, the fish swim in exuberant, synchronized happiness. As the exultation fades back into the day-to-day exploration for food, ROXANNE, the youngest fish, bursts out in a unique, expressive solo. Sheer joy overtakes her and she breaks from the group in a spontaneous display.*]

DORSAL: [*Admonishing her.*] Roxanne!

[*Sheepishly, ROXANNE conforms, and rejoins the others in their synchronization. They swim. After a moment, as they continue to swim, HERRY, the bottom fish, is struck with a thought.*]

HERRY: Say, do you remember Davy?

DORSAL: Davy?

HERRY: Yeah.

DORSAL: What'd he look like?

HERRY: Like you . . . and him . . . and her . . . and me . . .

[*The fish think.*]

OTHERS: No. Nope. Un-huh.

HERRY: Hm.

[*They swim. After a moment, DORSAL comes once again across a morsel, eats it, and exclaims to the others with glee:*]

DORSAL: Smelt dung!

OTHERS: Smelt dung! Yea!!!

[*With added gusto, a feeding frenzy ensues. After the food is devoured, the fish swim in a particularly jubilant fashion. This sends ROXANNE into a frenzy, and as the other fish's exultation fades back into the normal day-to-day exploration for food, ROXANNE swims with unwavering delight.*]

DORSAL: Roxanne! [*ROXANNE continues to swim independent of the others.*] Roxanne! Stop that at once! There are no solos in the esprit de corps—it's a break of the sonar code.

ROXANNE: I don't care. I don't want to be like all of you. I want to be unique. I want to be a star!

GILL: There are no stars in school . . . only conformity.

HERRY: Otherwise, chaos! [ROXANNE *swims dangerously close to* HERRY.] Be careful! You might bump me, break my fin, and send me into a life of constant circles.

DORSAL: Roxanne, I implore you. Stop this at once. No good can come from this. [ROXANNE's *swimming slowly conforms to the others' and they swim once again in harmonious synchronization. After a moment,* HERRY *is again struck with a thought.*]

HERRY: Say, do you remember Daphne?

GILL: Daphne?

HERRY: Daphne. She particularly enjoyed ameba clusters.

[*The fish think.*]

OTHERS: No. Nope. Un-huh.

HERRY: Hm.

[*The fish swim.* ROXANNE *looks at the others. The need to express herself builds dramatically within her until she simply cannot hold it any longer. Eventually, she boldly and joyously swims independent of the others.*]

GILL: There she goes again.

HERRY: Dorsal, do something. She's going to draw attention to us!

DORSAL: Roxanne! Please, cease this foolishness.

ROXANNE: It's not foolish. It's who I am. It's an expression of me. I call it "Roxanne's Underwater Ballet." Isn't it beautiful? I've got to be true to myself. I don't want to be just like you—just like every other guppy in the sea. I need to be noticed. I need to be loved. I need you to love me for who I am. This is who I am. Love me. Love me! I am a star!

[*As she dances,* ROXANNE *is devoured by a large fish—one rung higher up in the food chain. The* OTHERS *scurry frantically in perfect synchronized terror to avoid being eaten. After the danger has passed, their swimming eventually fades back into the normal day-to-day exploration for food. A peace, a calm, and an understanding comes over the group. They swim. Then eventually . . .*]

DORSAL: Fame is fleeting.

[*They swim.*]

GILL: Her ballet was rather beautiful.

[*They swim.*]

HERRY: We'll certainly remember her. [*Pause.*] Won't we?

[*They swim. Then, in perfect synchronization, of course, they swim away, as the lights fade.*]

END OF PLAY

LITTLE MOM

Marc Palmieri

CHARACTERS
ANNA: *7 to 10 years old*
GIRL: *7 to 10 years old*

TIME
The present day.

SETTING
ANNA's *room, late afternoon on a school day. At rise:* ANNA, *dressed in her school clothes, stands with her arms folded, staring angrily at her closed bedroom door. A knocking is heard on the door from the other side that sounds like an adult's knocking.*

ANNA: You can knock all you want, Mom! I'm NOT coming out! I'm staying in my room FOREVER! You'll never see me again, until I'm OLD! OLD like YOU! [*More knocking.*] I'm not coming out to "talk about it," because all you're doing is trying to trick me into NOT BEING MAD! And I'm MAD! Do you understand? That kids get MAD? No! You don't! You don't understand ANYTHING, do you? Maybe you've never BEEN A KID AT ALL! [*No knock.*] Finally!

[ANNA *walks to her bed and sits on the edge. She begins to take her shoes off.*]

Such a beautiful afternoon to be outside. What a waste! Again! Every day. Same thing, with that fake, phoney, happy voice. "Come in, Anna! It's time!" Ugh! Don't parents know, it's not enough time! We go to school. All day! Reading, writing, math, science, social studies, blah blah blah! Lessons! Tests! Review! More tests! Ugh! We come home and we need to relax! Need to have fun! Play dates! Video games! Television! Snacks! Every afternoon should be a new adventure! But nooooo! All you get is enough time to START having fun. Then it's OVER!

[*Another knock on her door, but it's a softer knock.*] Go away, Mom! [*No knock.* ANNA *paces her room, talking out loud to herself.*]

Just when I'm getting my energy back, finally putting the long school day behind me, enjoying myself, WHAMMO! My mother's voice saying the same thing: "Come in, Anna!" or "Come downstairs, Anna!" Ugh! It's like I want to explode! "Come on, Anna! Time for homework! You got lots of homework! Then we have to eat! Then you have to take a bath! Then you have to brush your hair, brush your teeth, pack your bag, pick out your clothes!" UGH!!!! That's all she cares about! What kind of life is this??? Is there never any rest? Must all kids suffer so???

[ANNA *tosses her shoes on the floor. Another knock, softer again— like a child's.*]

All right. I'm tired of the knocking! You wore me down. Ruin my day some more! There's no lock on the door anyway! [*After a moment, a GIRL, similar to ANNA in age, enters. Her clothes are a little different, like maybe from just over thirty years ago or so.*] Who are you? I don't know you. Do I?

GIRL: Yes you do. No you don't. Well, kind of. Well, not really.

ANNA: Uh, that's confusing.

GIRL: Yes. It is.

ANNA: Ohhhkay. So what are you doing in my house?

GIRL: You do know me. Only you don't. And I'm always in your house. Well, not always.

ANNA: That's totally creepy. I've never seen you before.

GIRL: Well, yes you have, but you didn't know it, maybe. I don't always look like me. Well, I never look like me, really. Not anymore.

ANNA: Look, I'm not in the mood for this. I'm mad. And I know I'll be spending the rest of my day and night doing hard, boring homework and getting myself ready for yet another school day.

GIRL: You don't like school?

ANNA: Ugh. Every time someone asks me that I want to say "No." But I guess I do. But only when I'm there. Not when I'm home. When I'm here I just want to be free and have fun.

GIRL: Me, too. Believe me!

ANNA: But I can't be free! Because I'm a KID!

GIRL: Me neither! Because I'm NOT A KID!

[*Pause.*]

ANNA: Huh?

GIRL: Huh?

ANNA: What did you say?

GIRL: I said I'm *not a kid*!

ANNA: Uh, yes you are.

GIRL: Uh, oh no I'm not.

[*Pause.*]

GIRL: Part of me is.

ANNA: You're confusing again. Please go.

GIRL: I will. But I can't go far. You see, I'll always BE here, in this house, or wherever you live. But just not this . . . visible.

ANNA: Creepy again. Hey, wherever you came from, go back!

[GIRL *takes a step further into the room, looking around.*]

GIRL: So weird. Even though you've seen a place a million times, it's so different when you look at it from a different angle. Like, if you lie on the floor in the car and look up? Or, stand on the coffee table and look down at the sofa? Or, come into your child's room and . . . ?

ANNA: Wait. What did you say?

GIRL: So weird. Even though you've seen a place a million—

ANNA: No. No. Not that part! The last part! "Your child's room"?

GIRL: Oh. Yeah.

ANNA: You don't *have* a child. You *are* a child!

GIRL: Well, not *all* of me! This is only part of me. I came from downstairs after I . . . your mom, well, stopped knocking and went down to the living room to feel sad.

ANNA: Huh?

GIRL: You yelled, "You've never been a child at all!" and she heard you. She hadn't thought about me for a while, but you made her remember. By the time she got downstairs, there I was—right in her memory.

ANNA: *Totally creepy!*

GIRL: See, I'm your mom when she was a child.

ANNA: *That* explains your weird clothes!

GIRL: Hey, I like my clothes! My mom worked hard to pay for these!

ANNA: Wait. You are my mom?

GIRL: Yes! Or who your mom *was*. Now, I'm just a part of her. A part that never gets much of a chance to be free. Kind of like what you were saying about your afternoons! Can I sit down?

ANNA: Uh . . . yeah. Sorry my bed's not made. Sorry my shoes are on the floor. I threw them.

GIRL: I don't care. I didn't even notice.

ANNA: Wow! You always notice!

GIRL: You mean I *will* notice, when I'm older. Just like you'll notice, when you're older and *your* child won't make her bed or put her shoes in a place where she can find them in the morning. You'll see! [GIRL *sits on the bed.*] What a great bed! [*She stands on it.*] Bouncy too! [*She starts jumping on the bed.*]

ANNA: Hey! Careful!

GIRL: [*Not stopping.*] Why? Bouncy-bouncy!

ANNA: Stop! She'll hear you!

GIRL: Who?

ANNA: Mom! I mean, *you*! You always tell me not to jump on the bed! Now *you're* doing it!

GIRL: I am!

ANNA: You could get hurt! That's what you always say!

GIRL: That's because I *did* get hurt!

ANNA: What?

[GIRL *stops jumping a moment.*]

GIRL: I was like eight or nine. I was jumping on the bed, just like this! I lost my balance and I jumped off the bed and hit my head! It was awful! I passed out and had to go to a hospital! And everyone was terrified, including me! [*She starts jumping again.*] WEEEE!

ANNA: Then what are doing!? Stop it! Mom! Stop! Stop now! I don't want you to get hurt!

GIRL: But it's fun!

ANNA: I know, but the hospital isn't fun!

[GIRL *stops*.]

GIRL: Aw, you're a party pooper.

ANNA: No I'm not. I'm just saying be careful. Especially since you *know* you can fall.

GIRL: Well, I guess I do know that. In fact, I always think about it. I think about all the things that happened to me when I was a kid. Falling, being afraid, not knowing things that are important . . . it makes me worry, now that I'm grown up. Worry a lot.

ANNA: Why? You're not a kid anymore.

GIRL: But you are.

[*Pause.*]

ANNA: Huh.

GIRL: You see, when you get big, when you grow up, the kid is still in you. You'll always be a kid. Only, you can't be. There's too many things you have to do. So even though you *want* to be a kid, you have to give it up all the time. [GIRL *steps off the bed.*] Yes. You think I don't love to see you have fun and be free? You bet I do. I remember how it feels. But I also know what comes after being a kid. And so I worry. And so I make sure you do the important things, even when you yell at me.

ANNA: Huh.

GIRL: Anyway, I gotta go. I'm grown up and have dinner to make and my own homework to do for my job. It never really ends. You'll see.

ANNA: That's bad news. I don't want to grow up. I want to stay this. Me.

GIRL: Oh, I want that too. Believe me. It's just not possible.

[GIRL *heads for the door.*]

ANNA: Well, 'bye, I guess.

GIRL: Thanks for letting me in. This was fun, even if it was just a few minutes, to be a kid with you.

[*She opens the door.*]

ANNA: Will I see you again?

GIRL: Um, maybe if you look real close, into her eyes, you'll see me. And when she laughs. Sometimes you can hear me when she laughs. But it's hard.

ANNA: What about when she's telling me to do my work? And ruining my day. And being a party pooper?

GIRL: It'll be hard. But remember. Without her, you might just keep bouncing and bouncing until . . . you know.

[GIRL *exits.* ANNA *stands there a moment. She looks into a mirror hanging on her wall. After thinking about something, she smiles. She moves to her bed and tidies it up, then puts her shoes together, neatly. She walks to her door and opens it.*]

ANNA: Mom! Mom? Thank you, Mom!

[*Blackout.*]

END OF PLAY

MY SISTER AND ME IN 1993
Ten Minutes of Biography
Sharyn Rothstein

My Sister and Me in 1993 was originally produced at the Ensemble Studio Theater in 2008. Abigail Zealy-Bess directed, and the cast was as follows:

SHARYN: Anna Aronson
MARISA: Quincy Confoy

CHARACTERS

SHARYN: *12 years old; a budding young poet who is a tad dramatic.*

MARISA: *7 years old; SHARYN's adoring younger sister and best friend (whether she knows it or not).*

TIME

July 13, 1993.

SETTING

SHARYN's *bedroom.* MARISA *sits down to write in her journal.*

MARISA: July 13, 1993.

[*Twelve-year-old* SHARYN *takes the stage and writes a letter.*]

SHARYN: Dear Children's Anthology of Poems: Hi! My name is Sharyn Rothstein. It's been my name for as long as I can remember. I'm twelve years old and I have a seven-year-old sister, Marisa.

MARISA: Sharyn has been telling me what to do, like "go get this," "put this in my room," "give this to Dad," "give me this," and I always do it—but sometimes she has to wait and then she starts saying "just give it to me" and when I ask her to do something she always says "you do it" and when I ask her to sit in her room she always says "no."

SHARYN: People say that I am a very deep thinker. I suppose I am, because sometimes things I think are so deep that even I cannot understand them.

[MARISA *sticks her head in* SHARYN's *room.*]

MARISA: Can I sit in your room?

SHARYN: No.

MARISA: Mom said you got mail.

SHARYN: Where is it?

MARISA: Downstairs.

SHARYN: Go get it for me.

MARISA: No.

SHARYN: Do it.

MARISA: You do it.

MARISA: No.

SHARYN: I said do it!

MARISA: Okay.

[*She leaves.* SHARYN *resumes her letter.*]

SHARYN: I have this idea that all people were made to think deeply, but I have discovered that since thinking deeply takes so much time and often takes fun out of life that some people have simply decided (before they were born) not to be deep thinkers. I speak of deep thinking as a disease, because I believe it is. I'm a deep thinker and my thoughts are practically running my life and I'm only twelve! But enough philosophy. I write to you in regard to a poem I have penned called "Last Will."

[MARISA *reenters with a letter.*]

MARISA: Can I sit in your room?

SHARYN: No. Give me my mail.

[MARISA *doesn't.*]

MARISA: What are you writing?

SHARYN: Another letter to get my poetry published. It's really important. So give me the mail and go away.

MARISA: I want to watch you write.

SHARYN: Ew. No. Give me the mail.

MARISA: Rob Golden made Tracy Dembicer go into the boy's room.

SHARYN: I don't care.

MARISA: I wrote something about you at school today. Mrs. Mellon made us write about our favorite superhero and I wrote about you and Critter.

SHARYN: Critter's a cat.

MARISA: So?

SHARYN: So a cat can't be a superhero.

MARISA: What about Cat Woman?

SHARYN: Cat Woman's skinny. Critter weighs more than Grandma.

MARISA: So?

SHARYN: So have you ever heard of a fat superhero?

[MARISA *thinks on this.*]

MARISA: But you can still be one, right?

SHARYN: OH MY GOD I AM TRYING TO WRITE! Give me the letter and leave me alone! [SHARYN *snatches the letter out of* MARISA's *hand. She tears open the letter and reads it.*]

MARISA: I don't think Critter weighs more than Grandma. Grandma's really, really fat.

[SHARYN *looks up from her letter.*] What?

SHARYN: I got rejected. Okay? Will you just leave me alone now?

MARISA: What's "rejected"?

SHARYN: Rejected. It means "rejected." From this magazine thing I sent my poem to.

[MARISA *takes the letter and tries to make sense of it.*]

MARISA: Dear Young Writer: Thank you for sending us—

SHARYN: OMIGOD—don't READ IT.

[*She sniffles.*]

MARISA: Want me to get Mom? She'll yell at them.

SHARYN: That's not the way it works.

MARISA: Oh. But just 'cause they didn't like it, somebody else might like it. Right?

SHARYN: [*Very dramatic.*] I don't know. Maybe I should just quit now. Maybe I'm just not a good writer.

MARISA: I think it was a good poem.

SHARYN: You never even read it.

MARISA: But if I did read it, I'd think it was good. Is this it?

[MARISA *pulls the copy of the poem out from the envelope.*]

SHARYN: Give it back. I don't want anybody to read it ever again.

[MARISA *dodges her.*]

MARISA: "Last Will" by Sharyn Rothstein. Like somebody named Will?

SHARYN: No! Jesus. Will. Like a will and testament. Like what Mom and Dad will leave for us when they *die.*

MARISA: What do you mean, when they die?

SHARYN: Ugh, you'll never understand it.

MARISA: [*Reading.*]

Last Will.

Do not step on me.

I am no smaller than you,

though you are blind and I can see.

Do not step on me.

I am no more dang- . . . dang-

[SHARYN *grabs the poem from* MARISA.]

SHARYN: Dangerous. I am no more dangerous than you,

though you are deaf and I can hear.

Do not step on me.

I am no more unkind than you,

though you are loud and I am mute.

Do not step on me.

MARISA: That's really good.

SHARYN: I'm not done.

Forgive my friends,

who trespass upon your disrespected land

in search of holy, untouched

once upon a time

forests.

And I will forgive you,

who have ripped me from my home

and killed my children
and ancestors
and self.

MARISA: Wow. I really like it.

SHARYN: I'm *not done!*
I beg of you only to spare me
for the future of your own
for should mine be gone
yours will be as well.
Remember me and my significance,
as this place dies,
and you die with it.
You are not a god.
Do not step on me.

    [MARISA *doesn't respond.*]

SHARYN: That's it. That's the end.

MARISA: It's *really* good.

SHARYN: They didn't think so.

MARISA: It's the best poem I've ever heard.

SHARYN: Really?

MARISA: It's better than the tree poem Mom always says.

SHARYN: Anything's better than that tree poem. That doesn't make me feel better.

MARISA: I think it's *really* good. I think you should send it to another place, and they'll put it in a book.

SHARYN: I'm never sending it anywhere ever again.

MARISA: But if you do, I think they'll put it in. 'Cause if they don't they're really stupid.

SHARYN: I don't know.

MARISA: I like the part about don't step on me.

SHARYN: It's about the land and also children.

MARISA: It's a good part. Can I sit in here now?

SHARYN: I'm still working.

MARISA: I'll be quiet.

SHARYN: Fine. But you can't watch me write. It's creepy.

MARISA: I won't watch you. I'm writing too. In my journal.

[SHARYN *takes out her pen and starts writing again.*]

SHARYN: I hope you like the poem I have written. If you publish it I can stop thinking about it and write something else probably more deep, because the older I get the older my thoughts are. In closing, here is another poem I have written.

The babies in their mother's wombs have been taught

beforehand to fear the world in which they

are about to enter.

And they are crying within a wall of human life,

and their shrieks are muted by the felonies which their carrier

has committed.

[MARISA *reopens her diary.*]

MARISA: July 13, 1993. Sharyn Number 2. Sharyn and Critter are my superheroes, even though Sharyn says Critter can't be because he is fat. So now my hero is just Sharyn. She wrote a good poem and showed it to me even though it got jected and she was busy and said she wanted me to leave her alone. I don't know what I would do without her. I think she will be a great writer one day. Or a marine biologist who looks at sharks. I love my sister.

[*She looks up at* SHARYN, *beaming.* SHARYN, *totally oblivious, keeps writing.*]

END OF PLAY

THE NEW
INVENTORS CLUB

Mark Konik

CHARACTERS

KIRSTY: *a 5th-grade female student*
EVELYN: *a 5th-grade female student*
KARL: *a 5th-grade male student*
JAMES: *a 5th-grade male student*
The four students are all members of the New Inventors Club.

TIME

The present day.

SETTING

The play takes place in a classroom at an elementary school. The members of the New Inventors Club are sitting around a table.

KIRSTY: I hereby declare the second meeting of the New Inventors Club open. [*Everyone claps.*] In our last meeting we decided that everyone had to come up with an invention. So now for the exciting part, seeing what inventions people have brought along? Who wants to go first?

EVELYN: I'll go first.

KIRSTY: Great Evelyn, I love your enthusiasm.

EVELYN: This is my first invention and it didn't take long to come up with.

KIRSTY: Well, tell us what it is.

EVELYN: I invented a poem. And it goes like this:

Inventing things is fun,

Inventing things is great.

If I invented a time machine,

I'd be in another date!

KARL: That's a great poem Evelyn. It even rhymes.

KIRSTY: It's hardly an invention. How does it help anyone?

JAMES: It made me feel happy.

KIRSTY: But it's not really an invention.

EVELYN: I made it up, so it's an invention.

KIRSTY: Anybody got a better invention?

JAMES: I invented something that can help with transport and pollution.

KIRSTY: What a great idea. Transport and pollution are a huge problem. These are the types of problems our inventions should be solving. Not a poem that makes us feel happy. Tell us more, James.

JAMES: It's sort of like a car, only much bigger. It takes you from place to place and it stops along the road to pick people up. Then, when you're on there you can ring a bell and it will stop at a special stop. People could catch it to work and school, you could even catch it to the shops. There could even be a place for people to store their groceries.

KIRSTY: That's not an invention—it's called a "bus."

JAMES: No—it's called "A big car that moves lots of people and drops them off at places when they ring a bell."

KIRSTY: Didn't you hear what I just said? It's called a "bus." I caught one to school this morning.

JAMES: I don't know if you heard me right, but my invention is called "A big car that moves lots of people and drops them off at places when they ring a bell." It's quite a brilliant idea.

EVELYN: Yes, that's brilliant. You could maybe even have another level on the top, and it could be just like a double-decker bus.

JAMES: I didn't think of that. What a fantastic idea.

KIRSTY: This is not going well. We haven't come up with any new inventions.

JAMES: Yes—we've come up with a great poem, and I am pretty sure I've come up with a solution to the world's transport and pollution problems.

KIRSTY: They're not inventions. Inventions are meant to solve problems, and be brand-new ideas.

KARL: Well, what did you come up with?

KIRSTY: I invented the club and the name so I thought that was good enough.

JAMES: How is that an invention?

KIRSTY: We needed a name and I invented one.

EVELYN: I knew I should have joined the chocolate-eating club. I bet they're not being told that their invention isn't even real.

KIRSTY: What about you, Karl—what did you invent?

KARL: I invented a dance.

EVELYN: Cool, let's see it.

[KARL *gets up and dances. He provides his own sound track.*]

JAMES: That's the most amazing, fantastic dance I have ever seen. How did you invent that?

KARL: Thanks! I was just walking on the weekend and my arms started moving and then my legs started kicking and then the dance just came to me and I thought, what an amazing invention.

KIRSTY: None of these are real inventions.

KARL: I just showed you my dance. Do you want to see it again?

JAMES: Definitely.

[KARL *gets up and dances again.*]

EVELYN: Yeah, Karl! That's a brilliant dance. You should do that on TV.

KIRSTY: It's not an invention!

JAMES: I think that they're all inventions.

KIRSTY: An invention helps people. It makes life easier. An invention is like a helicopter or a new computer. Anyone can make up a dance or poem.

KARL: Anyone could make a helicopter. That's easy.

KIRSTY: So you think it would be easy to make a helicopter?

KARL: What did you think I did on the weekend?

KIRSTY: What, you built a helicopter?

KARL: Yep. But then I had to pull it apart because it wouldn't fit in our garage.

EVELYN: This is the worst club ever!

JAMES: I thought the New Inventors Club would be fun. But you keep saying that none of these are real inventions. When they're great ideas.

EVELYN: I quit!

KARL: Me too.

JAMES: I'm out of here!

KIRSTY: Wait, you can't just leave the club. It's a new inventors club. I like being in a club and hanging out with you guys.

EVELYN: Me too.

KARL: I'll miss you all.

JAMES: I love this club.

KARL: But you keep saying that none of our inventions are real inventions.

EVELYN: We could invent a new name for the club.

KARL: Great idea!

JAMES: I really like Karl's dance. Maybe we could change it to a Dance Club.

KARL: There is already a dance club . . . and besides, I still want to come up with new inventions.

EVELYN: I've got it. Why don't we call it the New Inventors Who Dance and Sometimes Write Poetry Club?

JAMES: Yes! I think that is the best invention of the day.

KIRSTY: Brilliant.

EVELYN: I think that there's only one last thing to do before we close the first meeting of the New Inventors Who Dance and Sometimes Write Poetry Club. Lead the way, Karl. We need to dance!

[*They all start dancing.*]

END OF PLAY

THE NO SOCKS GANG

Shirley King

A shorter version of *The No Socks Gang* was produced for *Gone in Sixty Seconds*, Brooklyn College, and University of Leeds, UK.

Lions, Tigers and Bears, a three-character version, was produced by Youth Education on Stage in Williston, North Dakota, in June of 2012.

CHARACTERS

HOLLY: *13 years old. She is worried about getting suspended from school for wearing Tigger socks.*

CAITLYN: *13 years old. She helps* HOLLY *come up with an ingenious plan.*

TIME

The present day.

SETTING

CAITLYN *and* HOLLY *are on the school playground.*

CAITLYN: Uh-oh. There's the bell. Will you hurry? We'll be late to Mrs. Turner's class, and you know what that means.

HOLLY: Detention. But that totally doesn't matter.

CAITLYN: What? Of course it does.

HOLLY: Not really. I think I'll just stay out here and kick a soccer ball around.

CAITLYN: Because . . . ?

HOLLY: I'm getting suspended anyway.

CAITLYN: Suspended! Why?

HOLLY: Look at my socks.

CAITLYN: You're wearing Tigger socks? Like Winnie the Pooh Tigger?

HOLLY: I can't help it. Our washer broke and these are the only clean socks I've got.

CAITLYN: You actually bought those?

HOLLY: My grandma gave them to me.

CAITLYN: Holly, you know the dress code. Solid colors only.

HOLLY: Don't remind me. I even searched my sister's sock drawer.

CAITLYN: And?

HOLLY: Totally empty.

CAITLYN: Well, maybe nobody will notice.

HOLLY: Trust me, Caitlyn, they will.

CAITLYN: I don't exactly get what they mean when they say "appropriate attire." Do you?

HOLLY: No way. I mean, these are just socks. It's not like I'm in a gang or anything.

CAITLYN: Come on, we'll be late.

HOLLY: You go.

CAITLYN: You're ditching?

HOLLY: I don't really want to ditch. Hey, what if I just sorta turned these socks inside out?

CAITLYN: So they're still striped but now they've got little strings and fuzz balls? I don't think so.

HOLLY: Any other ideas?

CAITLYN: Know what? Maybe we could use a black marker to cover the orange stripes. Give me your backpack.

[*Frantically looks through* HOLLY's *backpack.*]

HOLLY: If we had a black marker, which I don't. Give me yours! [*Grabs* CAITLYN's *backpack, pulls stuff out of it while* CAITLYN *shifts from one foot to the other, checks her watch, and tosses her hair in frustration.*] No marker! What if we ran back to your house? Maybe I could borrow a pair of your socks.

CAITLYN: And be late for Mrs. Turner's class? We're having a test today, remember?

HOLLY: I know! I actually studied for that test and she'll never let me make it up. You know how she is.

CAITLYN: Do I ever. No cell phones, no texting, no slouching at our desks. I think she'd be better at some other job.

HOLLY: Meter maid?

CAITLYN: Prison guard.

HOLLY: She's not all bad. Remember how she decorated our room just before winter break with the Holiday Duck Family?

CAITLYN: Fine, if you like ducks in Santa suits, and of course you do.

HOLLY: Well, yes. I mean, who doesn't?

CAITLYN: I can't stay out here much longer. I'm already late–almost.

HOLLY: Go to class. Caitlyn. No reason you should get in trouble just because my socks aren't right.

CAITLYN: How about this: what if you wear one of my socks and I wear one of yours?

> [*Flops down and begins removing her shoes and one sock.* HOLLY *does the same. They trade one sock each.*]

HOLLY: Oh, wait, this won't work. We'll both get suspended. Quick, think of something else.

CAITLYN: You know, they might as well make us wear uniforms.

HOLLY: Hello? We already do. Only solid colors? No patterns, no stripes, no pictures, no flowers.

CAITLYN: Isn't a dress code against our civil rights or something? Or do we even have civil rights as teenagers?

HOLLY: Well, I am really in serious trouble.

CAITLYN: Maybe you could just take off both socks.

HOLLY: You think?

CAITLYN: Or no, forget that. There's prob'ly some rule against it that we don't even know about.

HOLLY: Well, it's the best solution you've come up with so far. Quick. Stand in front of me.

CAITLYN: Why do I have to stand in front of you?

HOLLY: So Mrs. Turner won't see what I'm doing.

CAITLYN: How can she do that?

HOLLY: I think she's got eyes in the back of her head. Seems like it, anyway.

> [HOLLY *flops down and begins removing her shoes and socks.*]

CAITLYN: You can't go to class without socks, Holly.

HOLLY: Who says? I've never heard of a No Socks rule. Have you?

CAITLYN: Well . . . no.

HOLLY: Then it must be okay.

CAITLYN: Are you sure?

HOLLY: Worth trying, anyway.

CAITLYN: Know what? I'm taking mine off, too.

[CAITLYN *drops down and removes her shoes and socks.*]

HOLLY: Seriously? Better think about this. I mean, thanks and all, but you might get suspended, too.

CAITLYN: Might not come to that.

HOLLY: How come?

CAITLYN: We'll just tell her we're the No Socks Gang.

HOLLY: What?

CAITLYN: We could be this really cool gang. Think about it, okay?

HOLLY: SO—instead of getting into fights and trying to protect our territory, we'll just do . . . what?

CAITLYN: Not wear socks.

HOLLY: Cool!

CAITLYN: Let's race! How about this? First one there gets a re-ward—okay?

HOLLY: Reward? What reward?

CAITLYN: Well . . . I'm not sure.

HOLLY: I know! She gets to be boss of the No Socks Gang!

CAITLYN: Okay!

[HOLLY *and* CAITLYN *toss their socks in the air as they run toward exit.*]

END OF PLAY

QWENDOLYN'S GAMBIT
Alex Broun

Qwendolyn's Gambit was first produced as a part of *Heart Shaded Blue* at the Newtown Theatre in Sydney, Australia, in 2005. Directed by Wayne Tunks.

CHARACTERS
RAZZA: *7 to 15 years old, a Rook*
BRENDAN: *7 to 15 years old, a Bishop*
KEIRA: *7 to 15 years old, a Knight*
QWENDOLYN: *7 to 15 years old, the Queen*
PATTIE: *7 to 15 years old, a Pawn*
BELINDA: *7 to 15 years old, the Replacement Queen*

NOTE: Height is quite important in the play—QWENDOLYN *and* BE-
LINDA *must be the tallest, then* BRENDAN, KEIRA, *and* RAZZA. *PAT-
TIE must be noticeably smaller than the rest—she can be on her knees.*

TIME
Sunday afternoon.

SETTING
The corner of a chessboard. RAZZA, BRENDAN, KEIRA, QWENDO-
LYN, *and* PATTIE *stand on stage*—RAZZA, KEIRA, BRENDAN, *and*
QWENDOLYN *are in a line, with* PATTIE *in front of* RAZZA. *Their feet
are rooted to the spot, but they can move their upper bodies. As the lights
come up they all sway on the spot, trying to avoid something swinging
above their heads.*

RAZZA: Here he comes again.

BRENDAN: Ooh, he's a clumsy one, this one.

KEIRA: [*To* QWENDOLYN.] Watch out—he's coming for you.

QWENDOLYN: No, he's just hovering.

PATTIE: Where's he going now?

KEIRA: [*To* RAZZA.] Over towards you.

BRENDAN: Watch out!

RAZZA: Here he comes, great clodhoppers.

[RAZZA *ducks.*]

RAZZA: Ha-ha—missed me!

PATTIE: I think he got me.

QWENDOLYN: Are you sure?

PATTIE: I think so.

KEIRA: He'll have to move you then.

BRENDAN: But was it a real touch—or just a graze?

PATTIE: I'm not sure.

RAZZA: Well, get sure. I'm involved here.

PATTIE: I think it was a graze.

QWENDOLYN: You're safe then.

KEIRA: Is it tournament rules, or a friendly?

PATTIE: Or maybe it was a touch.

RAZZA: Make up your mind.

BRENDAN: All this uncertainty is quite off-putting.

PATTIE: I don't know!

QWENDOLYN: It's okay. He's castling.

RAZZA: Castling?

BRENDAN, KEIRA, AND RAZZA: Which side?

QWENDOLYN: King's side.

PATTIE: Whew! We can all relax then.

RAZZA: Not for long.

[*Slight pause.*]

KEIRA: Can anybody see? How we doing?

BRENDAN: Not too good. He's already lost a front-liner.

PATTIE: Which one?

QWENDOLYN: Mine.

PATTIE: Oh no—good old Pattie 5.

BRENDAN: I thought you were Pattie 5.

PATTIE: No silly—I'm Pattie 8. But don't feel too bad. We're identical.

RAZZA: Did he at least get one of theirs?

BRENDAN: Afraid not. Gave it up without even the slightest hint of a fight.

KEIRA: He's hopeless.

RAZZA: We're doomed! All doomed!

QWENDOLYN: Quiet now. It's early days. We all have to make sacrifices occasionally.

PATTIE: Did she say "sacrifices"?

BRENDAN: 'Fraid so.

KEIRA: [*To* BRENDAN.] Well you'd know all about those, I guess.

QWENDOLYN: It's all for the greater good.

RAZZA: Don't see what's good about it.

QWENDOLYN: We make an individual sacrifice so the rest may survive.

RAZZA: It's all very well for you to talk about sacrifices Miss La De Da, because it's not you who gets sacrificed.

KEIRA: How do you figure that?

RAZZA: Think about it—you got Rook's Gambit, Knight's Gambit, and Bishop's Gambit—even Pawn's Gambit—but whoever heard of Queen's Gambit?

PATTIE: What's a gambit?

BRENDAN: A sacrifice—he's talking about giving up your mortal role so the rest of us may live on.

PATTIE: Don't like the sound of that.

RAZZA: Well we all do it, my small friend—me, Brendan, Keira—even all eight of you. All except Miss Queen Qwendolyn.

QWENDOLYN: Do be quiet—he's about to make his next move.

BRENDAN: Probably botch it up again.

RAZZA: No, I won't be quiet. It's a travesty and I'm not putting up with it.

KEIRA: Actually, I have.

RAZZA: Have what?

KEIRA: Heard of a Queen's Gambit. I believe it's quite common, actually.

RAZZA: Crap.

KEIRA: It is.

RAZZA: Is not.

QWENDOLYN: I can assure you, Rachel—it does exist.

RAZZA: Don't call me that. My name's Razza.

QWENDOLYN: Well, Razza, I can assure you—there is such a thing as a Queen's Gambit.

RAZZA: Oh, yeah? How can you be so sure?

QWENDOLYN: Because I think he's about to play it.

PATTIE: Oh, Queen Qwendolyn—no. No!

[QWENDOLYN *jerks suddenly as if being pulled from the spot— she stumbles left then right then exits straight ahead and off the stage.* BRENDAN *mutters a blessing and crosses himself.*]

KEIRA: Oh, dear Qwendolyn—and so early in the game. [*To* RAZZA] And you—how rude and ungrateful.

RAZZA: Steady on, sister. She'll be okay. We all gotta get moved sometime.

PATTIE: Don't speak so quickly.

KEIRA: What's he doing? Don't leave her there.

BRENDAN: Can't he see my black counterpart? Oh my Grace.

RAZZA: [*Calling.*] Hey Dumbo—get her out of there!

KEIRA: Too late—he's released his hand.

BRENDAN: And our opponents see the mistake.

PATTIE: Oh no—Queen Qwendolyn!

[*They all hide their eyes and turn away. There is a loud crunching noise from off. They all flinch.*]

BRENDAN: [*Making the sign of the cross, giving last rites.*] In nomine Pater . . .

PATTIE: Poor Qwendolyn.

RAZZA: That bloody idiot.

KEIRA: He wasn't even looking.

PATTIE: Noble Qwendolyn.

KEIRA: I wonder which one of us will be next.

RAZZA: Always the Rook. Once the Queen's gone—I'm next in line.

PATTIE: Regal Qwendolyn.

RAZZA: Steady on Pattie 8—she wasn't all that crash hot.

KEIRA: Says you! Bloody useless. Stuck in the corner. Hiding.

RAZZA: I am not hiding. Just fenced in. You wait till I get out of here. I'll show them!

BRENDAN: Quiet now, sisters . . . Qwendolyn's passing has affected us all, but be assured that in the great land Off Board there is another life—one much greater than our humble existence here—where we will all live forever—in peace and harmony.

PATTIE: Even with the black pieces?

BRENDAN: Yeah, sister—even with them. And readily I say unto you, in the great world Off Board we may all live freely with no rigid constraints to bind us.

PATTIE: You mean no squares? Holy crap! Oops. Sorry Father.

RAZZA: Sorry your lordship, but you're missing the point. We're not that upset about Qwendolyn passing . . .

KEIRA: Hey! Speak for yourself.

RAZZA: We're upset about the fact that she passed so pointlessly—for diddly-squat.

PATTIE: Diddly what?

RAZZA: All because our guy is so bloody hopeless. She went to the Great Board in the Sky for nothing.

KEIRA: [*Watching.*] I wouldn't be so sure.

BRENDAN: Keira's right. Our opponent was so busy grabbing Qwendolyn, he's left his whole left flank exposed.

PATTIE: And our boy's on to it.

RAZZA: Go on son!

BRENDAN: He's moving fast now.

KEIRA: The other guy doesn't even know what hit him.

PATTIE: We may not even be needed.

RAZZA: Go on son!

BRENDAN: He's split them wide open.

KEIRA: Our opponent's pieces are shell-shocked.

PATTIE: Their king is exposed!

RAZZA: Go on son!

BRENDAN: Mate in two.

KEIRA: Does he see it?

PATTIE: Yes he does!

RAZZA: Go on son.

BRENDAN: One!

KEIRA: Almost there.

PATTIE: Two!

RAZZA: Go on son!

ALL: Checkmate!

[*They all clap and cheer.*]

RAZZA: Good on you, son. Well done!

KEIRA: Don't you mean "Good on you, girl?" It was Qwendolyn who won it for us.

RAZZA: Fair call. Gotta give her that.

BRENDAN: Yeah, you're right sisters. She did give up her mortal life so we may all live on in peace.

PATTIE: Yep, she was a bonza chick.

KEIRA: Thanks, Qwendolyn . . .

RAZZA: Wherever you are . . .

BRENDAN: Lest we forget.

[*Slight pause.*]

PATTIE: So, what do we do now?

RAZZA: I don't know about you, but I'm looking forward to a good nap. I'm tired.

KEIRA: For once we both agree. Let's get some sleep.

[*Suddenly,* BELINDA *enters.*]

PATTIE: Who's she?

BELINDA: Hello. My name is Belinda. I am your new Queen.

RAZZA: New Queen? We just got rid of the last one.

BRENDAN: Great King defend us!

PATTIE: What is it?

KEIRA: Look over to the other side of the board.

BRENDAN: The vanquished black pieces. They're reappearing. Regrouping.

PATTIE: What's going on?

BELINDA: For your eternal sacrifice—we are grateful.

RAZZA: Oh no!

ALL: [*Except for* BELINDA.] He's playing another game!

[*All the pieces sway on the spot, trying to avoid something swinging above their heads.*]

RAZZA: Here we go again!

[*Blackout.*]

END OF PLAY

SENSATIONALLY, YOU

Steve Koppman

CHARACTERS

MICHAEL: *15 years old.*
RUTH: *10 years old;* MICHAEL*'s sister.*
They are city kids, bright and literate for their ages.

TIME

The present day.

SETTING

A remote, pristine natural environment, at least from the perspective of modern urban people. MICHAEL *and* RUTH *look out across a lake at some hills.* RUTH *carries binoculars, which she looks through intermittently. She has a notepad and a big funny pencil sticking out of the back pocket of her brightly colored pants.*

RUTH: It's *so* beau-tee-ful.

MICHAEL: Yeah.

RUTH: It's just—*so*—beautiful. [*Pointing.*] Look at the snow up on the mountain.

MICHAEL: Yeah. Yeah.

RUTH: The lake. It's so *blue.*

MICHAEL: [*Looking at it, nodding.*] Yeah. Yeah. Really glad Mom let me bring you today.

RUTH: [*Gesticulating.*] There's so *much* sky.

MICHAEL: So glad you finally got to see Bear Mountain.

RUTH: It's so *perfect!*

[*Beat.*]

MICHAEL: [*With a slight touch of ambivalence.*] Yeah.

RUTH: You don't think so?

MICHAEL: No. I do. It's really beautiful.

RUTH: But you've seen *more* beautiful places?

MICHAEL: Oh, no. [*Shaking head.*] No, Ruthie. I don't—think so. It's really—awfully beautiful.

RUTH: So?

[*Beat.*]

MICHAEL: It's [*Beat.*] just—

RUTH: What?

MICHAEL: I don't know.

RUTH: You *don't know*?

MICHAEL: I'm not sure. I'm—

RUTH: Mikey!

MICHAEL: Sometimes when you say—some kinds of—things—they can—change—the way—how—other—people—see—things.

RUTH: What do you mean?

MICHAEL: I really like telling you stuff, but—sometimes—it's hard to know what's—good—to say.

RUTH: You mean like when you told me how Grandma used to chase Mommy and Aunt Muriel around the house with a hairbrush when they were little?

[*Beat.*]

MICHAEL: Well—yeah—maybe.

RUTH: Or—that stuff about [*Giggling.*] girls in your class?

MICHAEL: [*Nodding.*] Yeah. [*Beat.*] Maybe. Sometimes I think maybe I should be—a—little—more—careful.

RUTH: Did Mom or Dad say that?

MICHAEL: No. [*Beat.*] No.

RUTH: [*Trying to look at him through binoculars.*] This is getting like a Nancy Drew mystery. Like I was trying to figure out before you told me we were coming here. [*Beat.*] Come on, Mikey. Tell me!

MICHAEL: It *is* incredibly beautiful. I really don't want to—spoil anything—for you, Ruthie. Ever.

RUTH: What do you mean, exactly?

MICHAEL: I just don't know if—

RUTH: Mikey!

MICHAEL: It's—kind of—hard—to explain.

RUTH: Tell me!

MICHAEL: I've only told this before to Mom—and Doctor Stein, you know, the eye doctor. [*Beat.*] I *tried* to tell 'em. I don't really know if either of 'em had any idea what I was talking about.

RUTH: *What?*

MICHAEL: [*Hesitantly.*] This may not make any sense—okay— Look—it's like—when—I—look real hard—at anything—close— you know, like, with my eyes—it's kind of, like, inside everything, I kind of see—kind of—like, this motion—going around—this move- ment—inside my vision—bits—of—movement, like.

[*Beat.*]

RUTH: Bits of movement?

MICHAEL: I'm kind of used to it already. Almost. But not [*Beat.*] quite.

RUTH: Like—things moving [*Gesticulating.*] around?

MICHAEL: And—in a place like this—I guess—I just notice it more—'cause—everything's so beautiful, and—light—you know, still. You want to really be able to see everything—perfect—beauti- ful—the way it really is.

RUTH: [*Squinting, looking around closely, covering each eye quickly in turn.*] But what does it *look* like?

MICHAEL: [*Gradually gaining momentum.*] It's kind of hard to describe. I mean, it seems like a—kind of—movement, inside— things, more when it's darkish, less in the light, but motion, kind of floating around in the air—like—little—bits running around, but not—exactly.

RUTH: Little *bits* running *around? Really?*

[RUTH, *covering each eye in turn, looks out into the distance, with and without binoculars.*]

MICHAEL: So you know, especially when I just want to be totally seeing how beautiful something is—I wish they could just go away. So I could concentrate. And really see, feel it completely, what I'm really looking at, how beautiful it is, like, get lost in it. If something's totally in the sunlight, at the right angle, sometimes—it feels almost—like, for a second—the—movement—it kind of goes away—but—not [*Beat.*] quite.

RUTH: [*Squinting intermittently.*] That's so—*strange.* [*Beat.*] *Isn't* it?

MICHAEL: I dunno.

RUTH: How old—I mean—were you when you first saw this—stuff—about? [*Beat.*] I mean, [*Looking away, as if feigning indifference.*] you weren't *ten*—like me—right?

MICHAEL: [*Very deliberately.*] Oh, no. No. No. [*Beat.*] Maybe I was [*Beat.*] nine. Or—maybe [*Beat.*] eight. Yeah—it feels like—I must've been—eight. [*Rotating hand back and forth.*] Or—nine.

RUTH: [*Pulling out notebook and pencil and writing briefly but feverishly.*] But *not* ten?

MICHAEL: No. [*Shaking head.*] No *way.* [*Beat.*] I just have a very strong feeling—I couldn't have been ten.

RUTH: That's *interesting.* [*She is squinting and looking around energetically, then gradually settling down. Long pause.*] Isn't it great how quiet it is here?

MICHAEL: Yeah. Yeah.

RUTH: It's just like so—so quiet. Like we're totally alone. [*Looking all around with her binoculars.*] No one else in [*Excited.*] the whole wide world!

MICHAEL: Yeah.

RUTH: Isn't it *incredible*?

[*Beat.*]

MICHAEL: [*Without fully believing it, nodding.*] Yeah. [*Beat.*] Yeah.

RUTH: You don't think so?

MICHAEL: No, I do.

RUTH: You *do*?

MICHAEL: Yeah.

RUTH: But really *truly*?

MICHAEL: Well—yeah—I mean [*Beat. Rotating hand back and forth.*] Kind of.

RUTH: You've been places that are even *more* quiet?

MICHAEL: No. [*Beat.*] No. [*Beat. Shaking head.*] I really—
shouldn't—

RUTH: What?

MICHAEL: No. You know—like, sometimes—it's really not such a
good idea to talk about everything you know or you—think, or—
like—you—think [*Beat.*] you—know.

RUTH: Pretty please?

MICHAEL: This stuff won't do you any good. Believe me.

RUTH: I wanna know what *you* do, Mikey. [*Contemplating.*] What
would Nancy Drew do at a time like this?

> [*Pause. Environment should be as silent as possible.*]

MICHAEL: Okay. Listen. When we're completely quiet. [*Pause.*]
You hear that?

RUTH: What?

MICHAEL: That sound. Off in the distance.

RUTH: *What* sound?

MICHAEL: That distant—low—humming sound. [*Pause.*] Hear it
now?

> [*Beat.*]

RUTH: [*Looking confused.*] May [*Beat.*] be.

MICHAEL: It's kind of like this—very—low—humming sound.
It's almost like you can't hear it. But you *can.* It's like [*Very softly.*]:
"Hmmmmmm." [*Beat.*] Hear it now?

RUTH: I'm not—sure. [*Beat.*] I—think—I—thought—that was part
of the—silence.

MICHAEL: But it's different.

RUTH: But not *so* different?

MICHAEL: If it was really part of the silence, you couldn't hear it.

RUTH: But Mom always says, When you can't sleep, listen to the
silence.

MICHAEL: Right. How do you think I started *hearing* all this stuff?

She told me that when I was three. I don't think I ever heard silence again! [*Beat.*] You know at home sometimes, like at night, it seems completely quiet, but then *behind* the quiet, if you really listen, you can always hear stuff. [*Beat.*] *All* the time.

RUTH: *Really?*

[RUTH *is intermittently trying to listen intently, then scouring the landscape with her binoculars.*]

MICHAEL: It could be, like, in the kitchen maybe, or behind the walls. You go outside sometimes—even in the middle of the night when it's supposed to be quiet—but there's all these noises . . . sometimes you can tell where they're from but sometimes you can't. It could just be the wind, or foghorns, or the highway, or just some giant monster thing in the distance, humming or pounding or something that doesn't sound like anything you know. When you don't hear one thing, it's like there's always something *else* further away, or deeper, like, *behind* it. It's as if your ears are always trying to hear *something.* So behind all the sounds you know, it's like there's always another one, then another behind that, further away, and then even another behind that one.

RUTH: [*Holding her ears.*] *Behind* it? *Really?* I don't know about this.

MICHAEL: So when you're trying with all your might to listen to the silence, just when you think you're finally hearing it, what you thought was the silence turns out to be—the refrigerator! It never stops! Or maybe cars far away on the highway, on and on and on all night long—or water running somewhere—the pump of a generator or a bunch of plants blowing in the wind or even the racket from crickets rubbing their legs together like maniacs! (I learned about *that* at camp!) I'm not sure any more if you're ever really able to hear true silence. [*Beat. He seems exhausted.*] I don't even know what silence sounds like any more!

[*Beat.*]

RUTH: Are you *sure* about all this?

MICHAEL: Maybe. [*Beat. Shrugging.*] I don't understand it all. I wish I *could* hear the silence. And be sure that's what it is. And sleep better.

RUTH: But that now [*Pointing.*]—that's the wind, right?

MICHAEL: [*Turning.*] Yeah. That's the wind.

[*Beat. She writes something down.*]

RUTH: You sure know a lot—about—stuff.

MICHAEL: [*Shrugs, sadly.*] Maybe *too* much. Or not enough. Of the right things. I sure know I have trouble sleeping. [*Beat.*] As you get older—you know, things go wrong, too. You can find out too much that—doesn't do—you—any—good. [*Beat.*] I always tell you things I don't tell anyone else. Most people won't listen. If it's anything they don't know already. [*Beat.*] I hope we can always tell each other—stuff. Important—stuff. But [*Looking at her.*], you know how I get really worried about—things. I—I—just—wonder sometimes [*Trailing off.*] . . .

[*Pause.*]

RUTH: Maybe we should go soon.

MICHAEL: Really?

RUTH: Yeah.

MICHAEL: Already?

RUTH: May—be.

MICHAEL: How come?

RUTH: Haven't we been here a pretty long time?

MICHAEL: It doesn't seem so long to me. But we can go any time you want. [*Looking around.*] You're right, though. This place *is* magical. [*Looking out over the scenery, as if trying to fix it in his mind.*] I hope I always remember it.

RUTH: [*Nervously peering into the distance, covering her eyes each in turn, looking through binoculars while intermittently making special efforts to listen hard.*] I bet *I* will.

MICHAEL: How come?

RUTH: I don't know. [*Slightly annoyed.*] What *is* that sound?

MICHAEL: What sound?

RUTH: That sound. I hear it now.

MICHAEL: I told you I shouldn't say anything.

RUTH: But I hear it.

MICHAEL: Pretend like you don't.

RUTH: But I *do,* Mikey.

MICHAEL: *Forget* about it.

RUTH: But it's *there.*

MICHAEL: It won't do you any good. Believe me.

RUTH: Isn't it?

MICHAEL: [*Quietly.*] You'll be sorry.

RUTH: [*Starting to tear up.*] I'm *already* sorry.

MICHAEL: [*Mournful.*] Oh, no, Ruthie! Don't be sorry *yet!* You're much too young!

RUTH: [*In tears.*] Why do you always end up *telling* me stuff like this?

[MICHAEL *hugs* RUTH, *sadly. Pause.*]

MICHAEL: [*Voice shaking.*] What do you think of the way every-thing—*smells* here?

END OF PLAY

SHOW AND TELL

Jenny Lyn Bader

Show and Tell by Jenny Lyn Bader received its world premiere production at the "8 in 48 Idaho" Short Play Festival produced by the Treasure Valley Children's Theater on September 26, 2015. The play was directed by Jordan Peterson and starred Ethan Bass, Justin Ravago, Nichole Stull, and Elizabeth Timm. The Artistic Manager of the festival was Julia Bennett, the Submissions Coordinator was Valerie Baugh, and the Producer was Autumn Kersey.

CHARACTERS

ERIC: *10 years old; always prepared.*

BEN: *10 years old; an old soul.*

CLARISSA: *10 years old; ERIC and BEN's classmate, generally meek.*

MS. OPEFUL: *Their teacher.*

NOTE: The character of MS. OPEFUL is played by an actor who is the same age as the actors who are playing ERIC, BEN, and CLARISSA.

TIME

The present day.

SETTING

One morning in MS. OPEFUL's class.

Note: The playwright has imagined and transcribed a tune or two for the musical bit in the script and would be happy to share these tunes with you if you get in touch, but it is also possible to invent other music for those moments. Although the characters are three kids and one adult, the playwright encourages the use of an all-kid cast. She would like to dedicate this play to her brother, John Bader, who understands the string of life.

MS. OPEFUL: Good morning class!

CLARISSA, BEN, and ERIC: Good morning, Ms. Opeful!

MS. OPEFUL: Today is a special day, because I won't teach! [*Pause.*] You will!

[CLARISSA, BEN, *and* ERIC *look confused.*]

MS. OPEFUL: Since, as I told you last week, today is . . . Show and Tell!

ERIC: [*Smug, feeling in his pocket.*] Oh yes.

CLARISSA and BEN: [*Unprepared, horrified.*] Oh no!

[ERIC *puts his hand up in the air.*]

MS. OPEFUL: Who would like to start? [*She looks at* ERIC's *raised hand.*] Anyone else? [*No one else.* ERIC *waves his hand more frantically.*] Is Eric the only one who remembered Show and Tell?

[*As* ERIC *continues waving his hand all over the place.*]

BEN: [*To self/the audience.*] Okay, okay, okay. This is not my fault. I just forgot. She told us *last week*. That is a long time ago!

CLARISSA: Ohh, ohh, ohh! This is all my fault! I am in so much trouble! I could get kicked out of school. End up in a bad school. Have a bad life.

ERIC: Why is she so mean to me? Why won't she call on me? I've had this in my pocket all week. All I want to do is show! And tell! Pick me. Please?

BEN: Ms. Opeful? [*Helpfully points to* ERIC.] I think he wants to go first.

MS. OPEFUL: Mmm. How about someone else today? What about—*You*? Ben, come on up!

[BEN *stands in front of the class and stares out, terrified and lost.*]

BEN: All right. I brought something in for Show and Tell today. It's. A . . . a . . . a . . . thing.

MS. OPEFUL: A thing?

BEN: [*Trying to figure it out.*] A—a—not a thing. But a thing. A thin thing. A string thing. A string!

MS. OPEFUL: Where?

BEN: This is a string you can't always see. It's the string of life.

ERIC: Oh, brother.

BEN: The life string that follows us wherever we go.

MS. OPEFUL: What are you talking about, Benjamin?

BEN: Let's say I'm walking with Clarissa.

[*He pulls* CLARISSA *up to the front of the room. They speak in loud stage whispers.*]

CLARISSA: What are you doing?

BEN: I messed up! Just go with it!

CLARISSA: But . . .

BEN: Please!

MS. OPEFUL: [*Observing as they walk.*] Mmmm . . .

BEN: If I then run around her in circles . . . [*He starts running around* CLARISSA.]

. . . I get tired, because I'm being pulled by the string of life!

ERIC: No, you're tired because you're running around in circles!

[BEN *completes a third circle around* CLARISSA, *and then appears to be yanked backwards by an invisible string that was winding around as he circled her.*]

BEN: We don't see the string, but—aaaah—it's pulling me back! [*He stops.*] Best thing to do? Is go back the same way.

[*He runs three times around* CLARISSA *in the opposite direction.*]

Ahh! Much better.

[*The others watch, skeptically. He tries another example.*] Or let's say I walk this way between the two of them.

[*He walks between* CLARISSA *and* ERIC.] It's easier to come back the same way. [*He walks back on the same line.*] 'Cause I don't want to get tangled . . . with him.

[MS. OPEFUL, *puzzled, looks for evidence of the string.*]

Like I would be if I walked like this. [*Now he walks between* CLARISSA *and* ERIC, *but instead of coming back the same way, goes back the other way and appears to be pushed backwards into* ERIC, *held back by the now taut "string."*]

ERIC: Hey, get off me!

BEN: It's not my fault. It's the string.

ERIC: [*Sarcastic.*] The string of life.

BEN: We all bump into it.

[MS. OPEFUL *suddenly emits an exasperated high-pitched sound.*]

MS. OPEFUL: Eeeep!!!! [BEN *is alarmed. But she turns to* ERIC.] Eric Hammermint!

ERIC: Yes, Ms. Opeful!

MS. OPEFUL: You have always been the best student in this class!

ERIC: Thank you. I think so, too.

[CLARISSA *rolls her eyes at this.*]

MS. OPEFUL: And you always do good!

ERIC: Yes.

MS. OPEFUL: What are you doing now?

ERIC: I'm doing good. And I'm doing it well.

MS. OPEFUL: No. You are speaking during another student's Show and Tell time.

ERIC: Gosh, I'm . . .

MS. OPEFUL: That's not okay.

ERIC: *Sorry* Ms. Opeful, but . . .

[MS. OPEFUL *now turns to* BEN, *sharply.*]

MS. OPEFUL: Now Ben, I don't see this life string!

BEN: No, you don't.

MS. OPEFUL: And Eric doesn't see it.

ERIC: No, I *definitely* . . .

[MS. OPEFUL *snaps at* ERIC.]

MS. OPEFUL: I told you to be quiet!

ERIC: Yes ma'am.

MS. OPEFUL: Clarissa doesn't see it either.

[*A worried* CLARISSA *looks at* Ms. Opeful.]

BEN: No, but . . .

MS. OPEFUL: But! But. But . . . [*A beat. Then she seems suddenly intrigued.*] It seems it's there.

BEN: Oh, it is.

MS. OPEFUL: Tell us more about this . . . "life string." Is it there all the time?

BEN: It's . . . It's there more, the more we think about it. If you forget about it, you might step over it and not notice. [*He walks, crosses back over to where he just walked, and easily passes by the "string."]* But if it's on your mind? It's very much there. *[He walks, crosses back over to where the string would be, and trips.* MS. OPEFUL *looks at him. She is more convinced now.]*

MS. OPEFUL: *[With concern.]* My goodness! Are you okay? *[*BEN *nods.* ERIC *raises his hand.]* Yes, Eric?

ERIC: I have a question. It's more there, it's less there. But does it ever *show up?* Can you show us the string? It's *Show* and Tell, not *Tell* and Tell. I'd like to see it.

MS. OPEFUL: Good question. Ben?

BEN: Like I said, you can't always, um . . . see it . . . *[*CLARISSA *nudges him.]* But once in a while, a piece of it . . . shows up. *[He sees what* CLARISSA *sees. The laces of his sneakers, one white and one orange. He undoes the orange lace.]* Sometimes, like right now, part of it gets caught in an actual piece of string. So you can see. Like this.

ERIC: That's your shoelace!

BEN: No, this is my shoelace, when it's been hit by the string that's all around us! The life string. And look what's happened. It's turned orange!

MS. OPEFUL: Wasn't it orange before?

BEN: Are you . . . sure of that? Think back. Did I really have one white and one orange shoelace?

*[*ERIC, *bursting to talk, instead hits himself on the forehead to imply* BEN *is being ridiculous.]*

CLARISSA: Oh, wow! That's much more than a shoelace . . . *[*MS. OPEFUL *looks at her quizzically.]* I can see it now. May I? *[She takes the shoelace and rapidly starts making cat's cradle–like patterns and designs with it.* BEN *holds part of it. Lights play on it.]*

MS. OPEFUL: My, it's wonderful. Ben, we will all be much more careful from now on when we walk.

ERIC: Yeah, especially you without your shoelace!

MS. OPEFUL: Eric, it's your turn.

ERIC: Thank you, Ms. Opeful. During our school vacation, I visited Peru. I saw the Andes Mountains. And I brought back something to share with you today. *[He reaches into his pocket, quite excited and* *nervous.*] This here is a rare stone, a piece of sphalerite I found in Pachapaqui.

[*He is so nervous, he stares out at the class, stricken by stage fright, as he takes out a small gray object and places it in the palm of his hand.*]

MS. OPEFUL: "Sphalerite"?

ERIC: That's an ancient Greek word for "tricky rock." See, it's a rock that can trick you. It can look so much like other normal rocks you might find. But it isn't. It's sphalerite. It's special. A very unusual precious mineral. [BEN *scribbles a note to* CLARISSA *and passes it to her. She ignores it, pushing it back. As* ERIC *continues to talk inaudibly,* BEN *whispers to her.*]

BEN: Doesn't look like a rare stone. Looks like an old piece of gum.

CLARISSA: [*Quickly whispering back.*] Sssh!

BEN: Argh! I wish I'd thought of that. I had a piece of gum! [*Taking out an old piece of gum from his pocket.*] That would've been a lot easier. Do you know what I could've done . . . ?

CLARISSA: You're going to get into so much trouble if you keep talking!

MS. OPEFUL: Clarissa! Where are your manners! Are you speaking during Eric's turn? Has the whole world gone mad? You are usually such a quiet and kind child. Would you like to be sent to–

BEN: It was my fault Ms. Opeful. I talked to her. She was shushing me.

[*Everyone is amazed by* BEN*'s turning himself in.*]

MS. OPEFUL: I appreciate your honesty, Benjamin. May I ask what was so important that you felt the need to speak during Eric's time?

BEN: I was just saying how Eric's precious mineral looked more to me like an old rolled-up piece of gum.

ERIC: It *is* a rare mineral! And you are a dunderhead!

MS. OPEFUL: Eric! Sit down! Your Show and Tell time is over.

ERIC: Yes, Ms. Opeful.

MS. OPEFUL: That was interesting. Perhaps we can all learn from it. We can learn—that a special thing might look very ordinary.

Like an old rolled-up piece of gum. [ERIC *looks miserable.*] Clarissa. Your turn.

CLARISSA: [*Realizing she's in trouble.*] For Show and Tell, I, um . . . [*She grabs a pencil and erases* BEN*'s note to her and stands up.*] . . . brought this . . . [*She picks up the piece of paper.*] It is . . . not just a piece of paper.

MS. OPEFUL: [*Cheerfully.*] It *looks* like a piece of paper.

CLARISSA: Oh yes! But we just saw a precious stone looked like an old piece of gum.

ERIC: [*Annoyed, raising his hand as he asks.*] Where'd you get it?

CLARISSA: My family also was maybe going to visit Peru this break, or France, or Zambia, but we didn't. We don't really go anywhere. But sometimes we go to a . . . magic shop. This is a magic piece of paper.

MS. OPEFUL: What?

CLARISSA: If you just give it a chance—it does things. It sings and dances.

MS. OPEFUL: It does?

[CLARISSA *makes the paper undulate to a steady rhythm. As she does, she hums a simple tune to that rhythm, as if music is coming from the paper.* ERIC *rolls his eyes. As she pauses between phrases,* BEN *joins in on a low note, counterpointing her tune, harmonizing, helping give an impression of music from an unknown source. She holds the paper on its side, making it move and humming with* BEN *when she is not speaking.*]

CLARISSA: And floats along . . . it makes waves . . . and then suddenly it takes off . . . [*She lifts the paper upwards: it faces the audience. Then she flicks her wrist and it seems to be waving in the air, side to side like a flag. The sustained notes she was humming are heard simply played on a musical instrument as* BEN *continues humming and she continues speaking.*] It changes direction . . . changes shape . . . [*She makes the paper dance up and down, gracefully.*] . . . takes on colors . . . Look at it. Look again. Is it only white? Wasn't it plain a moment ago? [*Light shift: paper looks red, then blue, then purple, as music builds.*] But sing to it, listen to it sing to you, and it can do magic. [*Now* CLARISSA *lets go of the paper but remarkably it seems to stay aloft, as if connected to her hand by a thread or wire, a paper flag above her hands waving on its own, a paper dancer below her hands soloing. A swirl of lights and music, as the puppet-like paper seems to go off on its own ballet.]*

ERIC: *[In awe.]* It turned purple! Is that paper alkaline based?

CLARISSA: You know, it could be.

MS. OPEFUL: Fascinating! Now, if I hold it, will it do the same dance and song?

CLARISSA: Um, I think—it would, do a different one.

MS. OPEFUL: May I? *[CLARISSA hands over the piece of paper, scared. MS. OPEFUL fingers it like a Ouija board.]* Hmm . . . Nothing.

CLARISSA: *[Panicked.]* Well, sometimes it . . .

MS. OPEFUL: *[Feeling movement.]* Wait. *[A false alarm.]* No . . . no. *[Pause.]* Mmm. *[Suddenly, a delighted MS. OPEFUL starts singing a rock version of the tune CLARISSA sang, as she makes the paper dance on her desk as if its corners were feet and it were doing an extremely animated jig.]* Na-na-na-na-na-na-na-na-na-na! Na-na-na-na-na-na-na-na-na-na!

[Colored lights whirl, shadows are projected on the piece of paper.] Na-na-na-na-na-na-na-na-na-na! Na-na-na-na-na-na-na-na-na-na!

BEN: Ms. Opeful?

MS. OPEFUL: Yeaahh! *[They all start singing and dancing together, joyous. Even ERIC joins in. Then MS. OPEFUL, now out of breath, hands CLARISSA her paper back.]* That was a great class, kids. We should go to lunch.

BEN: *[As if disentangling himself from her.]* Okay, be careful of the string of life on your way out!

MS. OPEFUL: *[Nearly trips from the suggestion as she starts walking.]* Oooh-hoh-hoh! Thank you. Yes. You know what? We had such a good Show and Tell, let's do one again tomorrow!

[She exits.]

CLARISSA: *[Horrified.]* Again tomorrow?

ERIC: Clarissa, that was really interesting. I'd like to talk to you more about the chemical content of that paper. Ben, I can't believe you got her to think there was an invisible string that comes from us when we walk. That's seriously dumb.

BEN: Really? But it's right over here. You should be careful! [*He walks along and indicates along the floor where the "string of life" would be, the spot where he just walked.*]

ERIC: Whatever! [*He picks up his schoolbag and tries to walk over the imaginary line but he is too suggestible and trips despite himself.*] Aaaah! What *was* that?

CLARISSA: Who knows? Can you ever be sure?

> [ERIC *picks up his bag to see it's properly closed, checks the contents.*]

ERIC: Oh my goodness!

CLARISSA: Are you okay? What's wrong?

[ERIC *takes out a stone from the bag.*]

ERIC: This is it! *This* is the incredibly rare piece of sphalerite from the mountains of Peru! It's been in my bag this whole time.

BEN: Then what was the thing in your pocket?

> [ERIC *takes out the thing from his pocket and looks at it.*]

ERIC: An old piece of gum?

> [*He looks mortified. Then he starts to laugh. Then they all start laughing, then dancing together, with the paper, the gum, the sphalerite, and suggestions through movement of invisible strings between them. They add pieces of colored paper that float into the mix . . . It seems they are all friends now. Music. Lights fade.*]

END OF PLAY

THE SILENT ONES
A Short Play for Young Spellers
Catherine Castellani

CHARACTERS

LETTER K: *A consonant with a chip on his shoulder.*

LETTER W: *She is a happy consonant.*

LETTER L: *She is a dreamy consonant.*

LETTER B: *He is a pompous consonant.*

LETTER C: *A feline consonant, she is changeable and tricky.*

NOTE: Each letter wears its letter somehow on its costume: for example, a cape covered in Bs, a jeweled medallion W, etcetera. Ideally, costumes are like something out of The Three Musketeers' trunk: frilly tops, capes, hats, knickers on K for a visual pun. However, a simple felt letter will do.

TIME
The present day.

SETTING
The hideout of the newly formed Secret Society of Silent Consonants is a basement with properly "underground" qualities such as bars on the covered windows, exposed brick, and ratty, mismatched furniture. The door has a speakeasy window that can be pulled open and shut. The windows are covered in brown craft paper or parchment, blocking the view, and are secured with black iron bars. There is a round wooden table with four mismatched chairs center stage, perhaps a candle flickering on it. Smaller tables may flank it to the left and right, but give the main table plenty of room.

> *Lights go up slowly to reveal a cellar room hideout. Letter K is seated at the main table, brooding. There is a sound of howling wind and a clap of thunder. Then a knock at the door. K ignores it. Another knock. W enters from stage right. She confronts K.*

W: Someone is knocking!

K: I can hear that, W.

W: K! Knocking! K-N-O-C-K-I-N-G. Shouldn't you answer? You're a silent *K*!

K: Me, answer? A-N-S-W-E-R. You're a silent *W*. You answer it.

> [W *goes to the door and slides open the window cover.*]

W: Who goes there?

L: It is L.

K: L? She's not silent!

W: Quiet! You be silent! I'm doing this! What is your password, L?

L: "Walk." W-A-L-K. That's a silent *L*.

W: Oh, "walk"! And it starts with a *W*!

[*W opens the door joyfully. L enters. She is holding an elaborate mask on a stick before her face to shield her identity.*]

K: And ends with a *K*. Yes, W. You get so enthusiastic about regular consonants. May I remind you that this is a *secret* society of *silent* consonants? Only those letters that app ear silently in the English language may join.

L: Then I am in the right place. At last. At last I can be myself.

[*With great relief, L sinks into a chair and discards the mask.*]

W: How did you hear about us? How did you find us?

L: It was just a whisper. From H. In an herb garden. He was wandering about the lavender, and I asked him what he was doing there. He said, "Can't you spell 'herb'?" Of course I can! But seeing H, for a moment I forgot: H-E-R-B. And then he told me, just hinted, that there were others. Perfectly normal consonants by day with an entirely silent and secret identity by night. I had to find you.

K: I couldn't stand it, always being identified as the hard, aggressive "K" sound, when I know how sneaky I can be! It was like a knife in the gut every time I app eared in a children's book. Every time! "Kangaroo"! Never "knuckle"!

L: How many of us are there?

K: Few.

W: Well . . .

K: There can't be many, W.

W: D was very interested.

K: D?

W: Fudge, bridge, fridge. I told him I could hear a *D* in there. Don't you? It's not good enough to pass in some accents. It's got to be a regular thing, silent all the time.

L: In "bridge" I hear it. But "fudge"? Wait, what about "Wednesday"? D could have a case!

K: I'll decide that!

W: [*To L.*] The club is K's idea. He's touchy about it.

K: "Secret society"! Not a "club." A "secret society of silent consonants." Where's the secret, where's the mystery, where's the exclusivity, if all twenty-one consonants can up and join?

L: What if they have a password?

K: I'll decide that! And "fudge" is not going to cut it, not with me! D is not silent. [*A clap of thunder, a howl of wind is heard. K is sulking. There is a mighty knock on the door.*] I will handle this. [K *stalks to the door and pulls open the speakeasy window.*] Who goes there?

B: It is B. Let me in. I am a silent consonant seeking fellows.

W: What?

L: B is so pompous. First consonant and all.

W: Oh, so what!

K: I doubt very much that you're a silent consonant, B. Go away.

B: You doubt me?

K: I do.

B: I said, you *doubt* me?

K: I—wait!

B: D-O-U-B-T. Utterly silent. Now open this door. The wind is frightful.

> [K *opens the door and* B *sweeps into the room, swirling a great cap e with a flourish, and striking a pose. He is wearing a black Lone Ranger–type mask.*]

B: I was told there would be cocoa.

W: Yeah, yeah. I'll get it.

> [W *exits stage right.*]

B: This is quite a small gathering.

K: It's a secret society, B.

B: Well, I expect we'll be joined by G and H any time now. And there are bound to be others. Wait until they get their dictionaries out.

[W *returns with a tray and four mismatched cups and mugs of cocoa.*]

L: Thank you, W!

[*They all sit to enjoy cocoa. There is a slow, insistent knock on the door.*]

K: Don't answer it.

[*The mysterious knock is repeated.*]

L: Why?

K: I have a bad feeling about this.

B: Nonsense.

[B *stalks to the door, dramatically sweeps his cape back, and opens the speakeasy window.*]

K: B, sit down!

B: Who goes there?

C: Open the door. It is C, a most changeable letter, and indisputably silent at times.

K: NO NO NO!

B: Password?

C: "Muscle."

K: "Muscle"?

W: She's right. That's a silent C: M-U-S-C-L-E.

L: That's right. We're right next to each other, and you never hear her.

K: Oh please, not C. She's the bane of my existence.

[B *throws the door open.* C *enters very slowly. She is wearing a long cape with a large hood that hides her face. She slowly lowers it.*]

C: Cocoa. Two Cs. Perfect.

W: I'll get you a cup.

K: No. Get her a mug. Nothing with C, please.

C: If I'd known you were here, K—

K: Oh, you knew all right! You're stalking me!

C: We're thrown together so often. Fate . . .

K: Shut up!

B: Rudeness, sire! C is certainly silent in "muscle"!

C: And "scissors." And "czar." Though T also claims "tsar," in the T-S-A-R alternate spelling.

K: T? We're going to have T in here!

[W *returns with a delicate cup of cocoa.*]

W: Sounds like T qualifies.

K: Ruined! My plan, my dream! All ruined.

[L, W, *and* B *enjoy their cocoa.* K *stalks downstage to avoid them all.* C *follows.*]

C: You knew very well I'd be here.

K: I suppose I should have thought it through. Yes. You find a way into everything.

C: Why don't you just admit you enjoy my company and drop the antagonism? You don't fool anybody.

K: I don't enjoy your company! I prefer to work alone! Don't you see? A secret society is about standing apart. It's about stepping away from the herd.

C: And banding together with your fellows.

L: It's not a society if there is only one member, K.

W: Admit it. You were lonely.

B: I say, K, y our cocoa will get cold. Join us!

[C *returns to the table, reluctantly joined by* K. *There are only four chairs, so* K *stands to drink his cocoa. He raises his mug to them all.*]

K: To the Silent Consonants of the English Language!

ALL: Bravo!

[*They sip. There is a knock at the door. All turn and look. Blackout.*]

END OF PLAY

TARRED AND FEATHERED

Claudia I. Haas

Tarred and Feathered was produced in July of 2014 by Youth Education on Stage in Williston, North Dakota. It was directed by David Gillam Fuller.

LEE: Willian Gergan
PAT: Libby Swensrud
KERRY: Paige Wold

CHARACTERS

LEE: *11 to 12 years old. He is determined to get his message of protest out to the world.*

PAT: *11 to 12 years old. He is* LEE's *extremely good-natured friend.*

KERRY: *11 to 12 years old. He is always connected.*

Characters can be either male or female.

TIME

The present day.

SETTING

A spring afternoon on a suburban street. LEE *is hiding in a yard in a chicken coop.*

[PAT *is calling for* LEE. KERRY *is texting.*]

PAT: Everyone's gone, Lee! You can come out!

KERRY: Whoa! That was a close one!

LEE: Is anyone *anywhere?*

PAT: No one's here. *Let's get going!*

[LEE *emerges. He is blackened with tar and covered in chicken feathers.*]

LEE: Don't laugh. [KERRY *uses phone to take a photo of* LEE.] And put away the camera! I don't need to be sprawled all over the Internet!

KERRY: But it's newsworthy!

LEE: Stop laughing!

PAT: [*Suppressing laughter.*] Who me? I wouldn't dream of it. [*Under his breath:*] Chicken.

LEE: What did you say?

PAT: Nothing—but you know—if it looks like a chicken and acts like a chicken . . .

LEE: There was a chicken coop in the backyard!

KERRY: Oh yeah. Everyone knows the Coopers keep chickens.

[KERRY *snaps photo.*]

LEE: I didn't! Give me that!

KERRY: That's my lifeline!

LEE: The world does not need to see me like this!

KERRY: We could become a media sensation! Hey—do the chicken dance and we'll put it on YouTube. Who knows? Maybe we'll get on TV!

LEE: Nooooo!

PAT: The feathers are stuck in the tar you got on the street—you know what that means, Lee?

LEE: Don't say it.

PAT: Tarred and feathered!

KERRY: There needs to be a record of this!

LEE: Don't make me smash the phone!

KERRY: No violence, please. Not healthy.

LEE: Look at me! I can't go home like this.

PAT: No one's home at my house. Except Mitzi, and she won't tell. She just barks. You can shower there.

LEE: What about your mom?

PAT: My mother's at her "self-help-healing-find-your-inner-voice-and-center-yourself" meeting. She never misses it.

LEE: Oh man, you two! What kind of friends are you? You were supposed to be my lookouts!

PAT: I was guarding you—from cars! I was looking up! Not down!

LEE: And where were you looking, Kerry?

KERRY: At my phone! I was texting Josh and Mary about the movie tonight. Somebody has to make plans.

LEE: Someone should have noticed they had just tarred the streets!

PAT: I was looking at the horizon for cars so you wouldn't get run over. One second I'm looking up the street, and the next moment you're screaming, "Hot bituminous, hot bituminous!" Didn't even know that was a word!

LEE: It means "asphalt"! Some people look out for their friends. Some people wouldn't let their friend crawl onto hot bituminous, burn themselves, and then leap onto the cool grass only to be covered in more . . . gross stuff.

PAT: Some people don't have friends that feel the need to write graffiti all over the street. Look at you—you're just a mess!

LEE: It's not my fault!

PAT: You're the one who crawled backwards into some freshly filled-in pothole and screamed . . .

LEE: It burned!

KERRY: Screaming did not help.

PAT: It brought people out to see what was going on, so *you* ran into the Coopers' yard—and backed into their chicken coop.

LEE: I was just trying to get out of sight!

PAT: It worked. You are now "unsightly!" Maybe you'll lay off creating graffiti for a while.

LEE: It's my way of warning society. You can't miss something written in the street.

PAT: You missed the hot tar!

LEE: Because you two weren't doing your job!

PAT: It was my job to keep you from being run over. I succeeded.

LEE: At least I have written my slogan "Fight Apathy! Or Don't!" on the street. Mission accomplished! Best slogan ever!

KERRY: I don't know what it means, but I'll defend your right to write it in the street.

LEE: It's deep, you know. Double meaning and all of that.

PAT: Cool. Unlike the street.

LEE: Don't remind me. So, I can use your shower? No one will ever know?

PAT: Yeah, sure—I told you I'd help you. You know, you could consider suing the city and getting some money out of it. I've heard of people doing that. Nothing was posted that the cracks were resurfaced with hot tar. They really should do that for people who want to sprawl graffiti all over the street.

LEE: Get real, Pat! How could I sue the city without my mother finding out? And how could I explain the feathers?

KERRY: Maybe your mother would understand. Maybe she'd want to sue. How many kids wind up tarred and feathered these days?

LEE: My mother would never sue! She's into this personal responsibility "take charge of your own life" stuff. I'll shower, wear your clothes home, and sneak in and change before she sees me.

PAT: Whatever you say. We'll have to use the towel we use when we wash Mitzi. Then I won't have to explain to my mother why the towel smells.

LEE: The dog towel???? I have to use a dog towel?????

PAT: And the soap would never work. I'll get my mom's nail polish remover! That stuff takes off anything.

LEE: *Nail polish remover?* We have a problem here, Pat! You can make me use the dog towel, but I draw the line at showering with nail polish remover!

KERRY: Pat's just being a good friend, Lee!

LEE: I guess.

KERRY: You know, it's a shame to not have a record of this. I mean—how many of my friends end up tarred and feathered? Just one photo?

LEE: No!

[KERRY *goes over and pulls a few of* LEE's *sticky feathers and attaches them to himself/herself.* PAT *notices and does the same.*]

LEE: What are you doing?

KERRY: Trying to look as silly as you! [*After* KERRY and PAT *feather their faces,* KERRY *poses with the phone.*] Come on, a selfie? Or selfies—of the three of us?

LEE: You just tarred and feathered yourself—for me?

PAT: We're in this together.

LEE: You're the best!

KERRY: We know.

[KERRY *holds up the camera and snaps a photo of the three of them as the lights fade to black.*]

END OF PLAY